A new book in
THE JOSSEY-BASS
BEHAVIORAL SCIENCE SERIES

COMMUNITY SURVIVAL FOR LONG-TERM PATIENTS

Mentally handicapped patients who have been hospitalized for long periods are increasingly being transferred to the community for treatment and rehabilitation. But available facilities are often inadequate and frequently prevent them from meeting the demands of the outside world. Although tens of thousands of these patients are now in the community, many will return to the hospital; others will be neglected or ignored. This new book shows how services and support can be provided for the long-term mentally ill to enable them to survive in the community.

Richard Lamb and his associates confront key issues that determine whether a mentally handicapped person can handle normal, every-day pressures and live as unsegregated a life as possible. They describe an individual therapy for patients that stresses practical issues of adaptation and the development of self-esteem; discuss a wide range of therapeutic housing arrangements; endorse a program that takes mental health professionals directly to board and care homes; show how day care treatment centers can be an essential resource for long-term patients if used primarily for

H. Richard Lamb
and Associates

Foreword by
Frank M. Ochberg and Lucy D. Ozarin

Community Survival for Long-Term Patients

crisis intervention; demonstrate how work can be used therapeutically; show how long-term patients can be helped to acquire social competence; explain the need for and techniques of program evaluation; and present a carefully thought-out bill of rights for users of outpatient mental health resources—rights that must be guaranteed to the long-term mentally ill if they are to truly participate in community life.

The authors have organized the available knowledge on treating and rehabilitating long-term patients into a coherent philosophy. Two guiding principles of their philosophy are that treatment should be primarily in the community and that serving long-term patients must be a high priority. Most chronic hospitalized mentally ill patients can live in the community if they are given the necessary support. This book shows what that support should be and how it can be effectively provided.

 Jossey-Bass Publishers

San Francisco · Washington · London · 1976

COMMUNITY SURVIVAL FOR LONG-TERM PATIENTS
by H. Richard Lamb & Associates

Copyright © 1976 by: Jossey-Bass, Inc., Publishers
615 Montgomery Street
San Francisco, California 94111
&
Jossey-Bass Limited
3 Henrietta Street
London WC2E 8LU

Library of Congress Catalogue Card Number LC 75-44883

International Standard Book Number ISBN 0-87589-274-4

Manufactured in the United States of America

JACKET DESIGN BY WILLI BAUM

FIRST EDITION

Code 7602

The Jossey-Bass
Behavioral Science Series

THE AUTHOR

H. RICHARD LAMB, M.D., is associate professor of psychiatry, University of Southern
California School of Medicine. He is the
senior author of *Rehabilitation in Community Mental Health* (Jossey-Bass, 1971)
and senior editor of *Handbook of Community Mental Health Practice* (Jossey-Bass,
1969).

Foreword

One Sunday afternoon in 1841, a volunteer named Dorothea Lynde Dix went to the East Cambridge, Massachusetts, women's jail to teach a Sunday school class. She was appalled. And what she saw there—the mentally ill thrown into jail with criminals, and all of the prisoners uncared for, untreated, and unclothed—she saw again in almshouses and jails throughout the state.

Miss Dix's outrage led her to begin a campaign for prison reform and the establishment of hospitals for the mentally ill that ultimately evolved into the social reform movement of the late nineteenth century. States built new "asylums" that provided humane, moral treatment for the mentally ill. But after several decades, the conscience of the country somehow ceased to function again. The mentally ill received less than custodial care.

A series of scientific, social, and political developments have spurred the mid-twentieth-century movement from custodial institutionalization to community-based care. Drugs such as phenothiazines, increased mental health manpower, improved mental hospital conditions, making the psychiatrically disabled eligible for monthly income maintenance, and the various federal and state community mental health acts all have contributed to this trend. State hospital populations have been reduced by more than half; in addition, six hundred community mental health centers have been approved for federal support. The balance has been tilted in favor of community care, and now more treatment occurs in the community than in state institutions. However, much still remains to be done. Many severely handicapped psychiatric patients released from mental hospitals and now living in the community cannot find the social, financial, vocational, medical, or psychological supports that they need for survival. It is about these handicapped people that Dr. Lamb and his coauthors write. When psychiatric patients are institutionalized, their needs are met, at least those which institutionalization does not extinguish. When these people return to the community, gaping holes in our systems of care are exposed.

We do not know how many former mental hospital patients are now living in the community. We know that the resident population in public mental hospitals in 1955 numbered 558,000 and now numbers less than 215,000. We know that these hospitals have admitted and discharged over 400,000 patients a year during the same period. We know that readmission rates to these hospitals have ranged from 30 percent to 60 percent. We have scattered figures to show concentrations of former mental patients. In one California county in which a state hospital is located, 10 percent of the people constituting the county's population of eighty-seven thousand are said to be former mental patients. In Long Beach, New York, the city government passed an ordinance to bar further placement of mental patients in the old resort hotels because the townspeople saw these people as a detriment to the community.

Deinstitutionalization has brought problems even though it was meant to be a humane effort to restore people to more normal living situations. In many places, handicapped people have been placed in communities without adequate resources or arrangements to help them meet the exigencies of daily life. Mental patients, especially those who are dependent and regressed by long hospitalizations, often have lost the skills that would enable them to obtain needed services and remain out of the hospital. This book addresses itself directly and in detail to the provision of these needed services.

Community Survival for Long-Term Patients is an apt and descriptive title. This book deals with key issues that determine whether a mentally handicapped person can make it in the community: effective living arrangements; the acquisition of social competence; the therapeutic role and use of work; the utilization of community resources; and, most important, the means of helping an individual to develop and use ego resources and strengths to achieve a sense of mastery in life. The approach and methods described here are tested and researched. They can be replicated or adapted elsewhere. The "Bill of Rights for Citizens Using Outpatient Mental Health Services," written by a former state hospital patient who has seen the seamy side of the care system but who speaks with wisdom and compassion, rather than bitterness, is a guide for those who make and those who carry out mental health laws and policies. It is particularly timely in view of recent court decisions concerning right to treatment and the issue of involuntary commitment.

The Community Mental Health Center Amendments of 1975 (PL 94–63) require state mental health authorities to develop and carry out plans that will improve the quality of care in mental institutions, eliminate inappropriate placements in such institutions, establish and enforce standards for operation of mental health programs and facilities, provide assistance in screening persons at risk of institutionalization in mental hospitals, and provide follow-up care for those leaving mental hospitals. This new legislation has also expanded the requirements that must be met for federal funding of community mental health centers. Added to the mandatory inpatient, outpatient, emergency, partial hospitalization, and consultation services are seven new essential components. Three of these have direct bearing on services to long-term patients: assistance to courts and other public agencies in screening persons considered for referral to a state mental health facility; follow-up care for those discharged from a mental health facility; and a program of transitional halfway house services for those discharged from such a facility.

We now face the complex task of addressing the needs of severely handicapped mental patients while continuing to reform our basic care institutions and wading through an era of extreme economic uncertainty. The period ahead will not be easy. To carry out Public Law 94–63 requires new alliances among providers and consumers of mental health care, among communities, states, and the federal Government, and between public and private mental health services. Interagency liaisons must be forged. The conscience of the nation must be aroused again. The authors of this book have provided guidelines that will help us focus on one of the most difficult aspects of this task—securing a meaningful future in the community for long-term mental patients.

National Institute of Mental Health   Frank M. Ochberg, M.D.
Rockville, Maryland   Lucy D. Ozarin, M.D.
November 11, 1975

Preface

Throughout this book it will be noted that mental health professionals do not clamor to treat long-term patients. Even where such patients are given some priority, the general feeling is that little can be done for them. Moreover, even those in the mental health field who are most optimistic about long-term patients often are only partially aware of the body of knowledge available to treat and rehabilitate them. *Community Survival for Long-Term Patients* rests on the premise that such a body of knowledge exists and that it can be pulled together as a coherent philosophy.

Another problem is what Adolph Meyer referred to as a "Persistence of Barnumism in America: Showmanship, advertising to create an impression of importance and implant false ideas" (Lief, 1948). It is difficult to portray the treatment of long-term patients as glamorous and exciting. Thus, even a coherent philosophy for effectively treating them cannot readily compete with the more dramatic aspects of mental health or the latest fad in treatment. But this book was written in the belief that community mental health is beginning to mature to the point where its workers are willing to do what should be done as well as what meets their own personal needs.

The guiding principles that serve as the underpinnings for *Community Survival for Long-Term Patients* are set forth in the first chapter. Attention then turns to a more detailed look at the various facets of helping long-term patients survive and thrive in the community.

In Chapter Two, a point of view and rationale of individual therapy with long-term patients is presented. Although the chapter stresses a reality-oriented approach and the practical issues of adaptation, it also stresses the importance of understanding the long-term patient's individual psychodynamics. For the patient to achieve mastery is vital, and mental health professionals need to take account of the heightened self-esteem that comes with the patient's knowing he can cope with the stresses of the world. Clinical examples illustrate the various strategies and techniques advocated.

Chapter Three deals with the wide range of therapeutic housing arrangements that have been developed for long-term patients. The degree of envelopment of the patient by his housing facility is emphasized; the more caretaking that is provided by the facility, the higher the degree of envelopment. A central theme in this chapter maintains that the degree of envelopment should be the least possible, depending on the patient's needs. The discussion focuses on a continuum of resources ranging all the way from the therapeutic residential center (a locked, intensively supervised facility in the community) to satellite apartment arrangements and the Missouri Foster Care Program.

Chapter Four considers the problem of making board and care homes therapeutic. It takes the position that what is sorely lacking is a treatment program that brings mental health professionals to the residents in their board and care homes. If done well, such a program offers us an opportunity to create high quality therapeutic living situations for tens of thousands of long-term patients. A number of clinical examples graphically illustrate the process.

Chapter Five holds that the day treatment center can be an essential resource for the long-term patient, if it is used primarily for crisis intervention and if it is run with the philosophy that the patient's stay should be brief and that goals should be clearly formulated. The chapter then describes the specifics of treatment in this setting and how the center can become the nucleus for a community network of services aimed at the rehabilitation and management of long-term patients.

Chapter Six describes how work can be a central part of the

treatment and rehabilitation of long-term patients. It discusses the philosophy underlying the use of work, many of the techniques of work therapy and vocational rehabilitation, and many of the problems that have to be overcome so that work can be used therapeutically.

Chapter Seven deals with social rehabilitation—helping the long-term patient acquire social competence. It presents a number of different programs which all have a common thread in that the patients' direct contact is not with mental health professionals or paraprofessionals, but with persons such as teachers, volunteers, recreation department personnel, and college students. (Mental health professionals have an important role to play, but they should function only as consultants.) Another common thread is that all of these programs take place outside community mental health centers; the goal is to normalize, to the extent possible, the person's environment.

An exposition of the need for program evaluation, and some of the techniques and problems of such evaluation, are presented in Chapter Eight. The book then concludes on a powerful note with a carefully thought out bill of rights for users of outpatient mental health services—the rights we must guarantee to the long-term mentally ill if we mean for them to truly participate in community life. The epilogue recapitulates the guiding principles more formally, and examples to illustrate them are drawn from all of the chapters.

Although six authors have contributed to this book, it is intended to be more than a collection of diverse writings. In addition to his own chapters, the principle author has provided substantial input for the others, with the exception of the chapter by Priscilla Allen. And generally the authors share a point of view; it is this that lends cohesiveness to the book.

In conclusion, I want to express appreciation for the invaluable assistance of Sara Nichols in all aspects of the preparation of this book.

San Mateo, California   H. Richard Lamb
March 1976

Contents

Contributors

Priscilla Allen *writes and speaks on mental health issues and serves as a consultant to such agencies as The National Institute of Mental Health and the California Association for Mental Health.*

Marjorie B. Edelson, *ACSW, is community mental health program analyst, Local Programs Services Section, California Department of Health.*

Victor Goertzel, *Ph.D., is a consultant in program evaluation to the San Mateo County Probation Department and is in private practice in Palo Alto, California.*

H. Richard Lamb, *M.D., is associate professor of psychiatry, University of Southern California School of Medicine.*

Cecile Mackota *is supervisor, Vocational Services, San Mateo County Department of Public Health and Welfare, California.*

Richard A. Shadoan, *M.D., is medical director of the Westside Aftercare Program, is in the private practice of psychiatry, and is assistant clinical professor of psychiatry, University of California at San Francisco.*

Community Survival
for Long-Term Patients

1

H. Richard Lamb

Guiding Principles for Community Survival

The intent of this book is to present a definite point of view regarding community treatment and rehabilitation of long-term psychiatric patients. It is not our purpose simply to provide a review of the various schools of thought and approaches. Opinionated? Probably. Objective and knowledgeable? We hope so. But we feel that workers in this field need an overall, coherent philosophy. The reader may not agree with ours, but this book will have served its purpose if it stimulates him to develop a more definite philosophy of his own. Community mental health has never faced a greater challenge than that of meeting the treatment and rehabilitation needs of the many tens of thousands of long-term mentally ill persons who are now in the community rather than in state hospitals.

Survival in the community is what this book is all about. One can move patients out of hospitals, but, as Priscilla Allen so eloquently points out in the concluding chapter, that does not mean they are in the community. They may be as isolated from the mainstream of society in a board and care home or cheap hotel as they were on the back ward of the state hospital. Survival in this sense

1

means handling the normal pressures of life, having an opportunity to work and play as others do, and living as unsegregated a life as possible.

A guiding principle throughout this book is that treatment should be primarily in the community. Treatment in the hospital should concentrate on psychiatric first aid and reconstitution (May, 1969). Further efforts should then be made to identify the precipitating stresses and to set up a sound plan of community treatment and rehabilitation. This is in contrast to the ultimate goal of out-patient treatment, which is resolution of long-standing problems and minimizing intrapsychic discomfort. It is during this phase of out-patient treatment—not during hospitalization—that psychotherapy, social therapy, and rehabilitation are most likely to be helpful. Further, it has been shown (Anthony, 1972) that while most types of inpatient treatment innovations improve the patient's in-hospital behavior, these approaches do not affect posthospital adjustment as measured a year or several years later. What does make the difference in the patient's adjustment in the community, as measured by community tenure and vocational and social adjustment, is the services that the patient receives after discharge from the hospital.

The Inadequacy of Community Programs

A guiding principle for community survival is that *community mental health programs must give a high priority to serving long-term patients.* In recent years the mass exodus of long-term patients from state hospitals has been dramatic. For instance, in 1961 there were thirty-seven thousand patients in the California state hospital system; in 1975 there were fewer than six thousand. Both financial (it is cheaper) and philosophical (it is better) considerations have led to this dramatic shift of long-term patients from state hospitals to the community. Still another factor is an increasing recognition, both in and out of the courts, that persons should not be confined to hospitals without clearly defined reasons. Unfortunately, too few community mental health programs give high priority to the severely and chronically mentally ill in terms of providing treatment and rehabilitation programs for them. Some people are now saying that this movement of patients into the community was a mistake, that both the patients and the community were better off before (Arnhoff, 1975). But the problem, in our opinion, is not the shift itself, but the fact that too often little has happened aside from the movement of persons from one place to another.

This neglect is intertwined with issues of funding. For instance, it seems to us that, at the very least, long-term patients should have first-priority access to the funds saved by closing state hospitals. But these monies often seem to be allocated for everything but service for these patients. That it is possible for most hospitalized chronically mentally ill patients to live in the community has been demonstrated, provided they are given the necessary level of support and structure (Cumming and Markson, 1975). Further, state hospitals are expensive to run, and considerable expense can be saved by closing them. However, if an adequate level of community services is provided, the savings are not large and costs may even increase (Gunderson and Mosher, 1975). Community care should be provided because it is better—not because it is cheaper. If long-term patients are truly to have a bill of rights such as that set forth in Chapter Nine, then they must have access to every penny and more that would have been spent on them had they remained in state hospitals. It is our conviction that *long-term patients have a right to high-quality community treatment and rehabilitation.*

It is now becoming apparent that in the early years of emptying the state hospitals, the needs of long-term patients in the community were approached with a great deal of naïveté. Simple discharge from the hospital was seen as a major accomplishment in itself; little notice was taken of the fact that few, if any, treatment and rehabilitation resources existed, and even where they existed, hardly anyone was available to facilitate their use. That these patients could make progress and needed a whole spectrum of active treatment and rehabilitation services was insufficiently recognized; they needed more than just food and shelter in the community.

There was another facet to the naïveté of those in community mental health. That some patients might need a long term, locked, intensively supervised facility in the community was a foreign thought to many who advocated return to the community. "Those patients who need such a secure environment can remain in the state hospital," was the rationale. But the general feeling seemed to be that such patients were few and that community treatment and modern drugs would take care of most problems. More people are now recognizing that a significant number of severely disabled patients present major problems in management and can survive outside of the state hospital only if they have a sufficiently structured facility in the community. This arrangement need not be permanent, and the patient should be worked with on an ongoing basis to help him progress to a level of more independence and responsibility.

As long as the state hospital remains an easily accessible resource, community mental health centers are slow to develop community alternatives for long-term patients. Nevertheless, simply closing the hospital and placing the patient in the community does not automatically result in a proliferation of services for long-term patients (Robbins and Robbins, 1974). Our society seems fully as capable of neglecting them when they are in the community as it is when they are on the back wards in state hospitals. It should be added that despite official policy and widespread professional belief to the contrary, the custodial mental hospital is not a thing of the past and continues to exist in many states as a major form of state-provided mental health care (Fowlkes, 1975).

It is unfortunate, but in our experience a fact of life, that many community mental health programs will not offer long-term patients the opportunity to share in the good life of the community unless there is external pressure to make this come about. When there is a strong mandate from administrators of community mental health centers to emphasize services for the long-term, then programs will be developed. However, all too frequently, the pressure must come from without. An example is the California experience, where much of the development of services for long-term patients was the result of financial pressure from the state on local (county) mental health programs (Lamb and Edelson, in press). In this carrot and stick approach, county mental health programs were offered financial inducements by the state for reducing the state hospital population and developing community programs to serve these persons. At the same time, financial penalties were threatened for those counties which simply chose to leave their long-term patients neglected in the state hospitals. Although it would have been better if the initiative had come from the local programs themselves, and in some cases it did, this policy did result in a wide range of services being set up to prevent persons from becoming state hospital patients and to serve former state hospital patients in the community, so they would not have to return to state hospitals (Langsley & Barter, 1975). These services included precare houses, halfway houses, satellite housing, aftercare, social therapy and vocational rehabilitation programs, and consultation to residential care (board and care) homes. Lest the reader be misled, in California as everywhere else, much more needs to be done, in terms of both quality and quantity of services. But one major accomplishment has been a change in community mental health centers—their personnel, at both administrative and staff levels, have an increased confidence in their ability to work with long-term patients and an increased interest in doing so.

Community mental health is committed to primary prevention and treatment of life crises. While few would quarrel with this statement, the corollary is often low priority and a low status of services for the long-term patient (Hogarty, 1971; Kirk and Therrien, 1975). It is frequently said that little can be done for long-term patients as compared with motivated persons with neurotic and characterological problems. It may be that underlying such rationalizations is a disinclination and even a distaste for treating long-term patients and a tendency to give priority overtly or covertly to bright, verbal, educated persons who appear to be the most likely candidates for insight through individual and group psychotherapy, persons with whom therapists feel they have much in common. One mental health center faced with the influx of long-term patients even set up a "task force on morale problems" as a result of the large numbers of chronic patients "clogging" their treatment system. It has been difficult for community programs to realize that both objectives can be accomplished: that treatment and rehabilitation of long-term patients on the one hand and programs such as prevention and crisis intervention on the other can coexist.

Another guiding principle of community mental health is that *patients must receive much attention at the time of their first psychotic episode.* This requirement includes identification of the basic and precipitating problems, resolution of these problems so that the patient's life can be stabilized and future acute episodes can be prevented, and provision of rehabilitation and therapy so that the person can achieve mastery over all areas of his life. Still, it must be recognized that even with all these services, a number of persons will continue to need a network of supportive services for long periods of time (Smith, Kaplan, and Siker, 1974).

Long-Term Patients' Special Needs

Long-term patients are often described as marginal, socially isolated, vocationally inadequate, and possessed of exaggerated dependency needs (Simon, 1965). They lack self-confidence and the social know-how necessary to communicate with other people. They lack ego strength in terms of the ability to withstand pressure and to cope with the usual crises of life. Thus, they have a limited repertoire of problem-solving techniques and develop severe psychiatric symptoms when confronted with only a moderate amount of life stress. In many cases the long-term patient's illness may be a way of communicating his needs to other people and getting society to take care of him. Most long-term patients have a need for structure, and many require direction and control (Ludwig, 1971). All of these characteristics may become particularly apparent when a patient is discharged after many years of hospitalization. While his self-esteem may have been extremely low in the hospital, he probably rationalized or repressed the extent to which he was overwhelmed by the demands of the world outside the hospital and just how unable he was to cope with them. Discharge thus becomes an abrupt and traumatic confrontation with reality (Sandall, personal communication 1975). All the old fears and inadequacies are suddenly remembered. The experience is culture shock of the most painful kind.

Although all of the above points apply to many or most long-term patients and are important in understanding and helping them, it is equally important that we do not simply stereotype them in clinical terms. In recognizing the problems characteristic of the long-term patient, we must deal with each individual as an individual. Further, even while recognizing such problems as lack of ego strength and powerful dependency needs, we must not be patronizing.

The problems of the long-term patient may be further compounded by the effects of prolonged hospitalization. As described by Ludwig (1971, p. 192), "many patients experience a deterioration in work habits, a diminution in self-discipline, an atrophy in social skills, the avoidance of competitive situations, a passive rather than active orientation toward the satisfaction of their needs, and long exposure to an environment that places minimal demands and stresses on them. There is also a tendency for their value system to change. Ambition, success, and the dreams of youth begin to vanish and are supplanted by a resignation to the status quo and a nagging insecurity about their ability to cope outside the familiar hospital setting. To accentuate this feeling of social alienation even further, friendships evaporate over the years, family members die, family ties weaken, and numerous other roots to the original community begin to wither. In effect, the patients' emotional and intellectual lifelines to the outside world become progressively closed off." We recognize that many of the disabilities often attributed to institutionalization can in actuality be a product of the illness itself and the person's earlier life experiences. But the environment in which the person now finds himself also has a profound impact. We should not lose sight of the fact that the same changes described as a result of prolonged hospitalization can occur when a person is institutionalized in a facility "in the community" such as a poor-quality residential care home or is allowed to become overly dependent on a day "treatment" center.

Many community mental health workers expect little of long-term patients; instead, almost all of their efforts go to gratifying dependency needs. What is not understood is that we demean our patients when we treat them as helpless, inferior beings who can achieve nothing. Our message should be, "We will nurture you providing that you strive for personal growth." Recognizing that a person has limited capabilities should not mean that we expect nothing of him. Central to the treatment of long-term patients is the guiding principle that *high (but realistic) expectations must be maintained so that the patients strive to reach their full social and vocational potential even though this potential may be limited.* This principle maximizes their participation in the mainstream of the community, enhances their self-esteem, and generally improves the quality of their lives.

A graphic example is provided by patients who are in transition from a day treatment center to a vocational workshop and who spend one half day in each facility. The contrast in behavior is remarkable. Since behaving like a patient is not acceptable in the workshop, given the expected role of worker, the person behaves like a worker. But in the morning, at the day center, the same person is fulfilling the role of patient and acts like a patient, exhibiting symptoms and bizarre behavior never seen in the workshop the same afternoon.

Although it is important to expect a person to realize his potential, it is equally important not to expect more than he can realistically achieve, or we may be setting him up for another failure (Allen, 1975). High expectations are frequently confused with unrealistic expectations. For instance, many therapeutic housing programs require a full daytime activity outside the facility. But what if it is a struggle for the patient just to live outside of a hospital? And what if he cannot manage more than half a day a week in an ex-patient club? Even then, he may be able to tolerate only limited interaction, which allows him to maintain social distance from other participants. All too often, what is lacking is an accurate assessment of the patient's current capabilities and sufficient flexibility in the program to take account of his limitations. As a result, the patient is often asked to do more than is realistically possible for him to do at that particular time.

Frequently, the consequence of our having unrealistically high expectations of the long-term patient is that the patient is actually excluded from mental health services. His failure to meet these expectations is a painful experience and a further blow to his already low self-esteem. He feels embarrassed and humiliated, that he has let everyone down; to avoid a repetition, he flees the program. Or an agency proudly proclaims itself a high-expectations program. But what of those who cannot meet the expectations? The agency's reply is, "We will be happy to take him when he is ready." In either case, whether the patient has withdrawn or has not been able to meet the admission criteria, he has been excluded from the program in the name of high expectations. This frequent end result in community mental health is all too reminiscent of the long-term patient's fate on a state hospital back ward—he is denied the services he needs and then forgotten until the next time he causes an acute disturbance.

The pace at which the long-term patient is able to change or to improve is a slow one (Allen, 1974a). Frequently we forget this and push our patients too far too fast. Sometimes we are misled by a veneer of strength that exaggerates the patient's actual capabilities. Sometimes the patient or his therapist needs to deny the extent of the problem. Perhaps the parents have never accepted, and never let the patient accept, his limitations. Or, for the patient, anything short of quick success means he must be a failure like his father. Or the therapist overidentifies with his patient and loses sight of what are realistic goals and how fast the patient can move toward them. The long-term patient needs to learn to pace himself so that he does not attempt to accomplish in a given period more than he is able. His progress may be slow, but he, and we, must learn to accept this. Otherwise he may push himself, or be pushed, into a situation where the only escape is a flight back into illness. One of the most beneficial things we can do for a long-term patient is to help him see that he must pace himself and then to help him learn how.

Meeting Long-Term Patients' Needs

We must direct our efforts to giving the patient a sense of mastery—the feeling that he can cope with his internal drives, his symptoms, and the demands of his environment. No theme of this book is more important than this one. All the methods in this book —work therapy, social rehabilitation, individual psychotherapy, therapeutic housing programs that promote independence—are designed to help the long-term patient increase his ability to master and deal with both internal and external demands. With the development of mastery, the patient achieves not only a better adaptation to his world but also a significant rise in his self-esteem and sense of self-worth.

To attain our object, *we must work with the well part of*

the ego. Regardless of the amount of psychopathology in evidence, there is always an intact portion of the ego to which treatment and rehabilitation efforts can be directed (Lamb, 1971b). The goal is to expand the remaining well part of the person rather than to remove or cure pathology. The focus should be on the healthy part of the personality, the strengths of the person. Even though the pathology is left alone, when the healthy part of the personality is expanded, the person is better able to function (Beard, Goertzel, and Pearce, 1958).

This book's orientation is clearly psychosocial. But this does not mean that we relegate psychotropic drugs to a place of little importance; we see psychosocial treatment and drugs not as antithetical but as complementing each other. However, since the introduction of the modern psychoactive drugs, many mental health professionals have had difficulty achieving proper balance in their use. On the one hand, some professionals have tended to overuse drugs and virtually anesthetize their patients. Drugs have been used for the convenience of staff, as a means of overcontrol, and also as a substitute for needed interpersonal interaction and caring. These problems, along with the lack of periodic review of medications, have adversely affected the quality of care in both hospital and community settings, as will be vividly illustrated in Chapter Four. On the other hand, other professionals have been reluctant to use drugs. This equally serious problem is diminishing; there is now widespread recognition that phenothiazines and related compounds, as well as the flowering of the psychosocial approach, have played a leading role in making possible the revolution in treating psychiatric patients that is known as "community mental health." Drugs also provide crucial ego supports for the patient in dealing with both the routine stresses and the crises of life. Still, some therapists continue to hesitate to prescribe drugs. Some of it has to do with the notion that change should take place through insight and the interaction of therapist and patient or of therapeutic milieu and patient. Concern about patients becoming overly dependent on drugs is another factor. Some therapists have objected to measures that are only "symptomatic." Still others fear that the use of psychotropic drugs will result in a deemphasis on the psychosocial approach. All of these arguments have some merit, but they seem like academic luxuries when a therapist watches his patient become progressively more psychotic and in need of hospitalization while the insight he is waiting for becomes full-blown thought disorder (Lamb, 1975). The evidence is now overwhelming that the use of psychoactive drugs has not just a significant but a striking effect on the relapse rate of schizophrenic patients (Prien, Cole, and Belkin, 1968; Hogarty and Goldberg, 1973).

Much attention should also be paid to the housing situation of the long-term patient. Chapter Three, "Alternative Living Arrangements," emphasizes the significance of the degree to which the resident is enveloped by his housing facility. The more the facility takes care of the patient, the higher the degree of envelopment. A guiding principle is that *the degree of envelopment should be the least needed and the patient's living situation should be as noninstitutional as possible.* This principle recognizes that people's needs change and that responses must change appropriately. For instance, if a high envelopment facility is needed, the patient should not be forgotten there; rather, he should be worked with to prepare him for a living situation that is more in the community. Residential care facilities (formerly called board and care homes) have the potential to be high-quality therapeutic living situations for many thousands of long-term patients. We recognize that to achieve such a massive transformation will, in many instances, require years of effort and will clearly necessitate a basic reorientation of priorities and resources. But a program of treatment, rehabilitation, and care that can be brought to such facilities and that directly involves mental health professionals can transform the milieu there into a therapeutic one. Another crucial ingredient is training for the facility administrators and a change in their orientation so that they are better able to see the long-term patient as a citizen and as a person.

A theme that will run throughout this book is that *goals must be clearly defined in all aspects of treatment for each long-term patient.* Then efforts become purposeful rather than diffuse. Knowing what we are trying to accomplish enables us to focus specifically on how to reach our goals. In Chapter Five, "Gearing Day Treatment Centers to Serve Long-Term Patients," we shall see that this means establishing limited goals that can be accomplished in the time available. We shall also see the problems that arise when short-term, limited goals are not differentiated from long-term, more far-reaching goals. The result is that patient and staff become unclear about what the day treatment center should be trying to accomplish as opposed to what is more appropriate for aftercare. The center becomes a less effective resource and, lacking a clear understanding of its objectives, may keep the patient too long and foster undue dependency. In addition, we shall see the importance of clearly defined goals in such instances as a sheltered workshop and individual psychotherapy, both of which become more effective and meaningful when patients and staff identify realistic goals and work toward them.

Another guiding principle in this book is that *work therapy should be one of the cornerstones of community treatment of long-term patients.* This therapy must be more than simply exposing the patient to a work activity. Even if he will never reach competitive employment, there must be an ongoing process of vocational rehabilitation. Much of the benefit of work therapy derives from the continual attention to upgrading and improving the patient's work performance and work skills. Moreover, we must avoid setting up a self-fulfilling prophecy by predicting that a patient, even the least likely one, will never reach competitive employment. If we see every long-term patient as having the capacity for improvement, we leave the way open for an end result that may surprise us. For many long-term patients, work is the only avenue out of the mental health system.

Yet another crucial principle is: *Persons who have been labeled as mental patients need to learn, and should be permitted to regain, the status of "normal community residents."* For instance, helping the long-term patient acquire social competence, a process usually called social rehabilitation, should be given a high priority in the spectrum of services for long-term patients. There should be an emphasis on social rehabilitation programs where the patient's direct contact is with nonmental health professionals—teachers, volunteers, college students. Insofar as possible, input by mental health professionals in social rehabilitation should be limited to consultation, the rationale being that bringing patients into contact with regular members of the community will lessen their feeling that they can associate only with other patients and persons specifically trained and paid to take care of them—as was the case in the hospital. This approach is consistent with one of the most important guiding principles of services for long-term patients, that *normalization of the patient's environment must always be a goal.* This means normalization not only of his social milieu, but of his living situation and his work situation as well.

In our zeal to promote community mental health programs to serve those who were formerly served by state hospitals, it is all too easy to lose sight of the fact that a patient can become as dependent on a community mental health center as he was on the hospital. Further, the process of labeling the person as a mental patient is reinforced rather than reversed. Not only do others continue to see the person as a mental patient, but the person himself continues to label himself as a person set apart. In Chapter Seven, "Acquiring Social Competence," we shall see how entire social rehabilitation programs can operate and be more effective outside of a mental health setting. For instance, to teach the basic skills of everyday living to long-term patients in one community, a program was set up, not only on an educational model, but actually in the educational system; recreation programs are run in recreation centers and led by regular city recreation staff. Mental health professionals are used only for consultation. Long-term patients begin to see that they can be like other people in the community, doing things that other people do, such as going to school or to a recreation center. By keeping long-term patients in mental health settings, dependency upon these settings, rather than independence, is promoted.

Having set forth the philosophy that underlies our approach to the community treatment and rehabilitation of the long-term patient, let us now examine in some detail the specifics of this approach.

2

H. Richard Lamb

Individual Psychotherapy: Helping the Long-Term Patient Achieve Mastery[1]

With the emptying of state hospitals, mental health professionals are being called on to provide community treatment to increasingly large numbers of long-term patients. Individual psychotherapy can play a central and key role, but first there must be a clearly understood point of view and rationale so that potential therapists do not turn away from the task in confusion and dismay. The long-term patient was seen and saw himself as helpless and incompetent in the state hospital. It is important not to dismiss him, in the same way, as being incapable of using psychotherapy.

The trend in the psychotherapy of schizophrenia in particular has generally been toward a decreasing interest in psychopathol-

[1] Some of the material contained in this chapter appeared in an article by the author in *Psychiatric Annals*, July, 1975, 5.

ogy and an increasing interest in practical issues of adaptation (Gunderson, 1973). The point of view expressed in this chapter is consistent with this trend. It focuses on reality rather than fantasy, on the present and the future rather than the past. It does not exclude, however, using the past to understand the present and predict what might happen in the future. Controversy exists as to whether regression is to be encouraged or discouraged in the treatment of schizophrenia; the assertion here is that it should be discouraged. The psychotherapy described in this chapter focuses on the exploration of the nature of the patient's problems and the kinds of stresses that precipitate them, as well as on the psychotherapeutic relationship itself. Exploration of both problems and the psychotherapeutic relationship are not seen here as conflicting approaches, but as two aspects of therapy that complement each other. Above all, achieving mastery is vital for the long-term patient because he gains heightened self-esteem when he knows he can cope with his illness and the demands of the world.

The kind of psychotherapy used with long-term patients does make a difference. Just putting patient and therapist in a room together for an hour a week does not automatically result in improvement for the patient. Whitehorn and Betz (1975) have shown that there is a very definite difference in the success rates of psychotherapy with schizophrenics depending on the style and techniques of the therapist; in this research, they found that successful therapists grasped the personal meaning and motivation of the patient's behavior, going beyond the mere clinical description and narrative biography. Likewise, these therapists more frequently selected goals aimed at helping the patient to modify his adjustment pattern in a specific manner and to use his assets more constructively, instead of seeking merely to decrease symptoms or focusing on psychopathology. The therapists with the lowest success rates tended to be passively permissive as contrasted with the successful therapists, who more frequently expressed their opinions about problems being discussed, expressed honest disagreement at times, sometimes challenged the patient's self-deprecatory attitudes, set realistic limits, and generally were more active in the therapy. The successful therapists conveyed to the patient a belief that he had a potential for independent action and thus for mastery of his environment and of himself.

This chapter describes psychotherapy in the community, not in the hospital. It has been shown that psychotherapy in hospitals can improve the patient's in-hospital behavior but does not affect posthospital adjustment (Anthony, 1972; Messier, Finnerty, and others, 1969). As a matter of fact, extensive and intensive psychotherapy in the hospital is likely to prolong hospital stay and increase costs (May, 1969). This is not to say that there should not be one-to-one contact between therapist and patient in the hospital. Such contact, like that described in Chapter Five in connection with day treatment centers, is essential in helping the patient to modify and resolve the precipitating problems that caused the hospitalization and in working out a comprehensive and appropriate aftercare plan. But psychotherapy, as described here, is best utilized after hospitalization. It is what happens after hospitalization that is crucial in determining whether the patient is able to remain in the community and improve his level of functioning (Anthony, 1972; May, 1969; Stein, Test, and Marx, 1975).

The effectiveness and relatively low costs of aftercare programs that center around social and chemotherapy should not blind us to the importance of one-to-one psychotherapy with long-term patients. Individual psychotherapy, particularly if it takes a here-and-now problem-solving approach, can be a potent therapeutic tool for which the social therapy aftercare setting cannot compensate. It gives the long-term patient the opportunity to develop the ability to better understand what kinds of situations are anxiety-provoking for him and to develop healthier ways of dealing with such situations. The patient-therapist relationship itself affords the patient an ego-corrective experience and an opportunity for growth by teaching him to trust and to tolerate closeness and by providing a testing ground where he may learn to express anger without losing control.

Insight Redefined

Insight is not to be neglected as a goal for the long-term patient. However, insight must be defined so that the therapist and his patient understand what their objective is. For the patient, insight means that symptoms such as delusions, hallucinations, and feelings that he is "falling apart" are understandable: the symptoms mean that he is under stress and is reacting to it. He is no longer overwhelmed by mysterious, frightening, all-powerful forces beyond his control, because the symptoms make sense. After helping the patient to see this much, the therapist works toward the recognition that logical, purposeful actions can follow from such insight. The patient must not panic, but must try to understand what the stress is that is producing the anxiety and hence generating his symptoms. Having identified the stress, therapist and patient next need to determine what actions need to be taken to resolve the problem. In the meantime, the patient must understand that increasing his medications will alleviate his symptoms and help maintain his problem-solving abilities. Insight is very meaningful in treating the long-term patient if the insight is here-and-now and reality-based—if, for example, the patient understands what kinds of situations are extremely anxiety-provoking for him and that there are certain ways to deal with or to avoid these situations, and if he considers how he interacts with family and friends and how these interactions need to be changed.

Case illustration: A forty-six-year-old, married woman had had numerous state hospitalizations for psychotic episodes over the past fifteen years. She had been out of the hospital for two and a half years, and although on fairly high doses of psychoactive drugs, she continued to have ideas of reference and, at times, paranoid delusions. When especially upset, she was certain that everyone was saying that she ate her own feces.

Many of her early weekly sessions with the therapist centered around helping her recognize these ideas of reference and delusions as symptoms, indicators that she was anxious and under pressure. She was at first skeptical, but since she had a positive relationship with her therapist, she was willing to entertain the idea. After four or five sessions, she was able to say, "I must tell you that I understand this on an intellectual level, but I'm not sure that I really believe it down deep. But I trust you, so I'll operate as if I really believed it." By examining her symptoms each time they occurred, she was able, with the therapist's help, to identify the particular stress that had precipitated them and to formulate a course of action that would resolve the situation. By dealing with the symptoms this way, she found that her life was becoming less chaotic and more enjoyable. Further, the situation was not being allowed to deteriorate to a point where the symptoms progressed to fixed paranoid delusions. It was only after six months of this kind of work in therapy that she was able to talk about the delusion of people saying that she ate her feces and in turn get some perspective on the fact that at such times her anxiety was especially severe. She was much relieved by being able to understand the symptoms as indicators of anxiety instead of experiencing them as very frightening feelings that seemed very real, very incomprehensible, and beyond her control.

A therapist, seeing his patient begin to decompensate under stress, will, of course, take some immediate action to intervene. Sometimes he can manipulate, or compromise with, the patient's environment to prevent or reverse this decompensation. But it is all-important that the patient be aware of the rationale for the action being taken and be as much a participant in it as possible. Eventually the patient can incorporate this active process of being aware of and dealing with stressful situations, based upon an identification with the therapist.

The Psychotherapeutic Relationship

The frequency and intensity of one-to-one therapy should be adjusted to the tolerance of the patient; it can be one hour a week, one hour every other week, half an hour a week, half an hour once a month, or whatever seems appropriate. Except at times of crisis, therapists should be very hesitant to see a schizophrenic patient more than one hour a week, because of the very real danger of developing a transference which neither the therapist nor the patient can handle. Schizophrenics generally have difficulty handling the closeness and regression that develop in intensive psychotherapy. To ignore this is to invite a transference psychosis (Fox, 1973a).

Case illustration: A thirty-two-year-old, married woman began outpatient therapy following a psychotic episode that had required hospitalization. It soon became clear that she had had a thought disorder and paranoid ideas for a number of years. In the first interview, she became extremely anxious and insisted that her husband be called inside from the waiting room. She was unable to explain what had happened but did ask that her husband be with her in subsequent sessions, and the therapist agreed. There were numerous problems in the marriage that needed to be discussed, and the patient seemed to feel free to talk about other problems in her husband's presence. On one occasion several months later, she arrived before her husband, again became very anxious, and again could give no explanation. From then on she and her husband always came together.

The therapy progressed well. After being seen weekly for several months, every other week for another six months, and monthly for a year, her visits were put on an as-needed basis. It was agreed that either she or her husband would call for an appointment if any problems arose that they could not handle together. This they did, coming in approximately once a year for a joint session. But about seven years after her first interview, the patient called and requested to come in alone. When she arrived, she reported that her life generally and her marriage were going well but that she had two special reasons for coming. First, she wanted to tell the therapist that her initial problem had been that she was afraid that she would lose control of herself and ask the therapist to have intercourse with her on the couch in the office. Second, she felt that she now had more control, and she wanted to be able to prove to herself that she could sit in the office with her therapist for an hour and maintain control, which in fact she did. Further discussion revealed that beneath the concern about sexual intimacy was a more basic fear of losing control generally and allowing herself to be dependent and "at the mercy" of another person in a close relationship. She had used her husband's presence to dilute the relationship with the therapist and, considering the amount of anxiety involved, had prevented what would very likely have become a transference psychosis.

Other techniques that keep the patient's anxiety at a manageable level can be employed where appropriate. Long silences should be avoided. Eruptions of unconscious material at a rapid pace should be discouraged.

Treatment of long-term patients is a long-term process. A frequent error is premature termination of therapy. This does not necessarily mean that the patient should be seen for an hour a week indefinitely. But with the long-term schizophrenic, there is no real ending (Mendel, 1975). The therapy may be reduced to once a month, or to twice a year, or to times of crisis only. For that matter, there may be a lifelong maintenance of the therapeutic relationship, even if there is only an occasional telephone call or perhaps no contact at all. But the memory of the therapy stays with the patient, who knows that the therapist is only a telephone call away.

Strengthening Ego Controls

There is a popular notion that if a therapist can help a patient to "express his anger," something very therapeutic has been accomplished. And indeed this is often true, especially with non-schizophrenic patients. But with long-term schizophrenics, a sudden explosion of anger may really be a psychotic loss of control that may lead to a further loosening of controls generally and quite possibly to a hospitalization. The amount of anger may be so intense and the amount of ego control so tenuous that one should tread with caution in this area. However, appropriate expression of anger over which the patient has control can be an important long-term treatment goal. On a short-term basis, one should be cautious, paying fully as much attention to the patient's ability to retain control as is paid to the underlying anger.

Case illustration: A forty-one-year-old man, a chronic schizophrenic, had been able to function quite well in a minor executive position between his infrequent psychotic episodes. Each psychotic episode, however, had been characterized by extreme anger and paranoia. In remission, he was a pleasant, friendly man with little overt hostility. He was universally described as a "nice guy." In therapy, each time the therapist allowed the situation to reach the point where the patient was expressing any real degree of anger, the patient began to decompensate. So, early in therapy (during the first few years), the therapist began encouraging the patient to suppress his anger, and each time the patient reconstituted and continued to function well.

As the relationship progressed and the patient felt more confident that his therapist would support him if he began to lose control, he began to assert himself, at first in small ways and later in more significant ways. It was a slow process, but after four years the patient was able to become overtly angry at his wife and more aggressive at work without losing control, disrupting his marriage, losing his job, or requiring hospitalization. He now has a feeling of mastery over his angry impulses that is very gratifying for him. Certainly his ability to be appropriately aggressive and at times angry without losing control has been a very healthy thing for him in terms of his own mental health and his improved relationships with his wife, employer, coworkers, and others.

A similar snare awaits the unwary therapist who tries to change the character structure of a borderline psychotic who has a saccharine exterior covering what is clearly a tremendous amount of underlying hostility. In the short-term, such a character structure is best left intact as a necessary defense against a psychotic loss of control over angry impulses. In some cases, changes can be effected over a long period of time. But often this character structure is so necessary to help a weak ego deal with an immense amount of anger that little or nothing can be done to change it even over a span of years. Therapists must content themselves with settling for what is possible. Not every person who walks into one's office can leave a well-analyzed person in tune with all his impulses and a model of mental health. Even though a character defense may annoy the therapist, it is far better than having a patient give up his defense and then become overtly psychotic.

Another way to help patients develop ego control is by encouraging them to confine their thinking to reality and preventing them from drifting off into ruminations about normally unconscious, primary-process fantasy. For instance, a woman with weak ego strength begins talking about a dream in which she had intercourse with her father. There is a great temptation here to get into a discussion of oedipal feelings, incestuous tendencies, and all the dynamics that easily flow from such a dream. A fascinating hour? Probably. But that evening or the next day, one is quite likely to have to deal with an overtly psychotic patient. One should not ignore such material but rather should help the patient to repress it. The therapist can say, "You love and miss your father, and sometimes it shows up in dreams like this. The sexual part of the dream disguises the feelings of closeness you had for him." If it seems desirable, patient and therapist can then discuss the father in reality terms. Or they can go on to some other pressing issue. As this procedure is repeated in therapy, the patient herself learns how to turn away from primary-process material, and, with her ego more intact, feels better equipped to grapple with the problems in her life.

The therapist can supplement ego control by setting limits on behavior: Don't stop therapy, continue taking your medications, don't impulsively quit your job. Often, retaining the therapist's approval is in itself sufficient incentive for the patient to adhere to limits set by him. Occasionally, the family can become involved in enforcing limits. At the outset, the patient is the passive recipient of the limits and passively complies. In successful therapy, however, by identification with the therapist, the limits are internalized, strengthening the patients' own inner controls and enhancing his ego functioning and his feeling that he can control his own destiny.

Giving Advice

Many long-term patients lack the ability to cope with the routine stresses of life. If these stresses are discussed in individual therapy, the patient may be helped to resolve problems that he cannot cope with alone. Sometimes the procedure is the same as that used with more healthy patients: the therapist acts as a catalyst, enabling the patient to identify the alternatives and choose the ones right for him. In other cases, the therapist may give direct advice. This may not come easily to the therapist, but it may be crucial for the success of the therapy. Sometimes the same advice has to be given over and over again to a patient, each time his maladaptive pattern of reacting to a particular stress is repeated. But it is hoped that the patient learns from the therapist new ways of handling situations and at the time of the next crisis will be able to arrive at the solution himself.

Case illustration: A thirty-six-year-old, married woman had been hospitalized five times for acute psychotic episodes between the ages of twenty and thirty-one. For the past five years she had been doing well in outpatient psychotherapy, with no hospitalizations and no overt psychosis. Her therapy, which initially had been once a week, was now once monthly. She was on vacation, visiting her mother in a distant city, when she called the therapist, obviously disturbed and in the incipient stages of a psychotic episode. Unraveling the story over the phone, the therapist finally ascertained that she had been going through her mother's cedar chest bringing out all kinds of mementos from the past. Finally she had come across a birthday card that she had received from her now dead father on her eleventh birthday, on which he had written, "Happy birthday to a good little girl who is doing the dishes on her own birthday." She was being flooded with memories of the deprivation she had experienced as a child, of the unreasonable demands that had been placed upon her, and of the feelings of loss for her dead father, about whom she felt quite ambivalent. The therapist's response was, "Put all those things back and close that cedar chest." The patient complied, and when she called back an hour later, she was much less distraught; she now felt in control of the situation and a psychotic decompensation had been averted. In succeeding visits over the years, she did not reopen the cedar chest either literally or figuratively.

Persons from the lower socio-economic classes, in particular, expect a professional to give advice, and the therapy may fail if advice is not forthcoming (Carlson, Coleman, and others, 1965). But nothing is more difficult for many therapists than to give direct advice and to give it in simple language without jargon. Nevertheless, the following example illustrates what can be accomplished if the therapist feels free to do things that are very different from what is usually described as psychotherapy. A middle-aged, chronic schizophrenic woman had first been seen by the therapist when she was hospitalized for a psychotic depression after her husband, unable to tolerate her hostility, her seclusiveness, and her alliance with her mother against him, had suddenly left her. He drove all the way across the continent, becoming increasingly overwhelmed by guilt with each mile. Finally he could stand it no longer and turned the car around and returned. The reconciliation in the hospital was not exactly a joyous one, but the patient went into remission, and following her discharge from the hospital, the marriage continued. The patient refused regular outpatient treatment, but has, over the years, called at times of crisis. Each time there has been direct intervention by the therapist, and the patient has not had to be hospitalized. The following is a typical example of one of these episodes. The patient, very disturbed and talking about suicide, called the therapist and requested an appointment. She could give no clear picture over the telephone as to what the problem was. The patient arrived for the interview with her husband, a burly, unsophisticated, but long-suffering and well-intentioned truck driver. A half hour of exploring all the known trouble spots in this couple's lives finally revealed the problem. The husband had been waging a campaign for the past year to induce the patient to go out more, spend less time with her mother, and have some social life; since she had no teeth, he had prevailed upon her to get dentures as a first step in making herself presentable in public. The patient repeated over and over again, "My dentures do not fit and so I am going to kill myself." Clearly what she meant was that she did not want to change her life-style, did not want to wear the dentures, and was very angry at her husband for attempting to force her to do so.

The therapist and the couple had been through this issue of the patient spending more time outside the home many times, and it had long since become clear that this seemingly iron-willed woman was not only unwilling but unable to change. The therapist now took a directive stance. To the husband he said, "Joe, I realize that these dentures cost a lot of money, and you really resent your wife not wearing them. I also realize that it really bothers you that your wife will not go out with you and spends so much time with her mother. But I don't think there's any way to change the situation. If you want things to settle down at home and the kids to be less upset and your wife not to end up in the hospital, I think the best thing for you to do is forget about the dentures and leave it up to your wife whether or not she wears them." The husband groaned, but seemed to recognize that it was a question of either accepting the situation or leaving again, which he was not psychologically prepared to do. He reluctantly agreed, and the patient responded, "Fine, then I won't wear them." The therapist said, "No, Roseanne, I don't think you should leave it at that. You should at least go with your husband to his union picnic. It's very embarrassing for him not to show up, year after year, and you owe it to him to attend and to make yourself look presentable when you do." She, in turn, groaned, but agreed to do this. She would not agree, as usual, to return for further discussion of these issues. A call from the patient a week later revealed that both parties had abided by their agreement and that the situation had returned to its usual unsatisfactory equilibrium. Despite their complaints, husband and wife both seemed to be able to live with the situation and even to derive some gratification from it. No more was heard from the couple until the next impasse, about eighteen months later. The patient no longer needs to become psychotic to resolve these situations; she knows she can call the therapist for advice and arbitration.

Frequently it is helpful to assist the patient to rationalize a situation and thus save face and self-esteem. Take, for example, a man for whom being in psychiatric treatment means that he is sick, an inferior person, and not really a man. Often these feelings can be dealt with in time, but for the moment the important thing is to keep him in treatment and his illness in remission. The therapist might say, "You know how concerned your wife is about you and how fearful she is you will have another breakdown. The more worried she gets, the more she upsets you, and the more preoccupied you become with the problems at home, the less you can function at work. So it really is important for you to remain in treatment to allay your wife's anxiety, to make her life more comfortable, and in the process to make your own life more comfortable." Of course, this should only be said if in fact the wife does have this reaction. Still, it is only a part of the picture. But it is a rationalization that helps the patient remain in treatment while retaining the self-image that is necessary for his psychological well-being.

Dealing with Life Problems

There is no substitute for the therapist's possessing maturity and an understanding of the very real problems of the life cycle (Lidz, 1968). The long-term patient's lack of ego strength results in an impairment of his problem-solving ability. Thus, much of psychotherapy with the long-term patient has to do with helping him handle the problems specific to that phase of the life cycle in which he finds himself. For instance, with adolescent patients, the therapist needs to understand the stresses of adolescence: the struggle for emancipation from parents and the conflict and ambivalence about becoming independent, the problems of identity formation, the difficulties of choosing a vocation, the task of achieving an adequate sexual adjustment, and the necessity of preparing to assume the responsibilities of an adult. Another example is what Marmor (1968) has called "the crisis of middle life." Marmor points out that in mid-life such stresses arise as the physical signs of aging, that is, the loss of hair and skin tone and the battle against weight gain, intimations of one's own mortality, and the deaths of friends and relatives. During this period, one very powerful stress for most people is recognition that they may never achieve the high goals they had set for themselves. And all of these stresses come at a time when there is the greatest demand on one's earning capacity to meet the needs of the family, including school-age children. The therapist must also understand the problems of reaching maturity, of graduation and going out into the world, and the feelings of uselessness and depression of the empty nest syndrome, when the children are grown and have left the home.

Although dealing with these kinds of problems may seem mundane to some therapists, it is central to psychotherapy, at least with long-term patients, who lack the ego strength to cope with these problems alone.

It is also crucial that the therapist help his patients deal with what Yalom (1975, pp. 5–6) has called "existential factors." These include:

> Recognizing that life is at times unfair and unjust.
> Recognizing that ultimately there is no escape from some of life's pain and from death.

Recognizing that no matter how close I get to other people, I still face life alone.

Facing the basic issues of my life and death and thus living my life more honestly, less caught up in trivialities.

Learning that I must take ultimate responsibility for the way I live my life, no matter how much guidance and support I get from others.

[Learning] what I cannot obtain from others. It is a harsh lesson and leads both to despair and to strength.

Yalom feels that most therapists are existential-oriented, often unbeknownst to themselves. At least this holds true for those therapists who help their patients.

Working with the Family

The family should be involved in the therapy on a regular basis, or at least as needed, so that the therapist becomes a person on whom the entire family can rely. Generally, however, and with long-term patients in particular, it is important to avoid contact with the family either in person or by phone without the patient being present. When the patient is not included, his fantasies as to what has happened "behind his back" run wild. He may think that the therapist and the family are planning to send him to a hospital. He may think that the family is winning over the therapist so that the therapist will take sides with them against the patient. He may think that the therapist is telling all his secrets to the family, and as a result he may be extremely hesitant about revealing himself further to the therapist. All of these fears may be avoided by taking a position with the family that the therapist will be glad to see them if the patient is present and gives his permission. In cases where the patient has strong objections to meetings with the family, but is not able to say no to them, it may be necessary for the therapist to tell the family that such meetings are not in the best interest of therapy at this particular time. However, considerations such as these must be balanced with the need to retain the support and cooperation of the family so that they will aid rather than undermine the treatment process. While the therapist's primary concern is with the patient, he must not be, or be perceived as, "against" the family. Moreover, the family may need help with their feelings of guilt about the patient's illness. Or a spouse may be ambivalent about continuing the marriage; here it is crucial that the issue be resolved one way or the other, so that either there is added stability at home or the patient and therapist know that new plans must be made. For these reasons the therapist may feel a family interview should be held despite the reluctance of the patient. The situation can be discussed candidly with the patient, who senses the problem anyway. The therapist should elicit from the patient his concerns about what might happen. He should tell the patient explicitly why he wants to have the interview and what, in fact, will be discussed. If there is some issue that the patient is fearful of discussing with the family present, and the fear is either legitimate or cannot be worked through, the therapist can say, "Fine, in that case we'll avoid that subject with your family." Assuming that it is appropriate to see the family, most patients can accept an explanation such as, "Your parents have a number of questions which they feel, rightly or wrongly, can only be answered by me. I feel that it is important that I not alienate them and thereby cause problems for the therapy. Rather, I would like to try to enlist their support. Further, there are a number of things that may be beneficial for us to explore together. In any event, you will be there to hear exactly what is said by whom." Some families attempt to circumvent this policy of seeing the family only with the patient present by calling the therapist and engaging him in long telephone conversations. A therapist should guard against being drawn into a conversation over the telephone that involves more than discussing a meeting with the therapist and the patient.

Another note of caution should be sounded. Many schools of thought implicate the patient's family in aggravating and even generating his illness. Thus, mental health professionals often blame and mistreat the family, through either open hostility or vague innuendo (Appleton, 1974). Badly treated families in turn retaliate in ways that are detrimental to the patient. They become less willing to tolerate the problems he causes, are less agreeable to changing their behavior toward him, and do not give information that would help the therapist understand him. We also must recognize that be-

ing the relative of a mentally ill person is traumatic and often overwhelming. Usually the family is already guilt-ridden and has a
sense of failure for having "produced a schizophrenic." Mental
health professionals must learn to treat families with sympathy,
understanding, and respect, in order to win their confidence and
cooperation.

Pursuing a similar train of thought, Arieti (1974) observes
that the schizophrenic tends to attribute to his parents full responsibility for his illness and his despair. Unfortunately, many psychiatrists have accepted these perceptions as real insights and as accurate
accounts of historical events. Arieti believes it is the therapist's job
to help the patient get his parents into perspective, by pointing out
how the patient distorts and exaggerates. "For instance, a white lie
is transformed into the worst mendacity, tactlessness into falsity or
perversion" (p. 587). Of course, the therapist must be careful, for
in some cases the parents have really been what the patient has
depicted. But usually when the patient comes to recognize that the
parents have played a role in his psychological difficulties, he also
exaggerates and distorts that role. He is not able to see his own
distortions until the therapist points them out to him. Further, the
patient must be helped to realize that negative traits of parents or
other important people are not necessarily arrows or weapons used
purposely to hurt him; they may simply be characteristics of these
people rather than attitudes directed solely toward the patient.
Arieti (1975) hopes that in psychotherapy the patient will stop
blaming others for all his troubles. He will recognize the role others
played in his life, but he will assume some responsibility for what
happened to him in the past and especially for the way he will direct
his life in the future.

Taking Sides against the Superego

Sometimes the best course of action is an attempt to modify
the patient's superego, thereby decreasing his guilt and the self-
destructive behavior prompted by this guilt. In other words, the
therapist takes sides against the superego. The patient may react
to certain situations in a self-destructive way because of lifelong,

inappropriate feelings of guilt, and the therapist not only must point this out, but must say, "That is self-destructive. Don't do it."

Case illustration: A thirty-one-year-old woman had received a constant message during her childhood from her parents and siblings that her role in life was to compensate for the failings of her alcoholic mother and take care of her father and her brothers. She had been made to feel that any gratification or enjoyment of life was wrong, that she should instead be devoting herself to the welfare of her family. As an adult, simply taking an enjoyable vacation was enough to overwhelm her with guilt and precipitate a psychotic break. One of the critical elements in the therapy of this schizophrenic woman was to encourage her to stop taking care of her parents and siblings, and to assure her that taking an enjoyable vacation, buying and enjoying a new house, and enjoying intercourse were not evil, but were in fact important for her to do, important not only for her but for the welfare of her own husband and children. Such intervention has not only helped this woman increase her enjoyment of life but has prevented a number of psychotic episodes and hospitalizations. For instance, early in the therapy, her therapist's statement "It's not wrong to enjoy a vacation" reduced her guilt and helped her both to enjoy the vacation and not to become symptomatic. But, for her, it was an external and foreign way of viewing the situation. As therapy progressed, the reduction in guilt became internalized, her superego became modified, and the patient became less dependent on the therapist to deal with and master what had been disabling guilt.

Guilt reduction can be extremely useful in a variety of ways. This point is illustrated by another schizophrenic woman, who felt a tremendous amount of resentment about the way her husband was treating her. She felt, however, that she was exaggerating the husband's behavior and that in any case she had no right to feel resentment. Her therapist had known the patient and the family for over ten years and was in a good position to assess the situation. His response was, "You are not at all exaggerating the way he is treating you. And it is a normal, human response to feel resentment about such treatment. Part of the problem is that your parents made you feel that all angry feelings are wrong. It is normal, it is all right, to feel resentful about this." By pointing out to the patient that her resentment was appropriate and reducing her guilt about the anger she was feeling, the therapist was helping her to see the realities in her life more objectively and to allow herself to have appropriate feelings about them. The result was a lessening of her depression and her need to use psychotic defenses to deal with her feelings of guilt.

Conclusions

These examples illustrate still another crucial point that is too often neglected in community mental health—the importance of understanding the individual psychodynamics of long-term patients. Aftercare programs consisting primarily of medication and social therapy, even when the relationships between the patient and the staff are good and there is close staff involvement, are often superficial. One can find a happy medium between the formal psychoanalysis of the schizophrenic patient and a program consisting only of medications and social therapy. It is important to understand the psychodynamics of the patient's illness, have at least a modicum of information about his early life, and in particular understand what kinds of real life situations interact with his internal dynamics in such a way as to cause a psychotic episode, interfere with growth, or deprive him of gratification from life. Mental health professionals must be able to combine the techniques of medication, social therapy, and individual and group psychotherapy based on a practical understanding of psychodynamics. They need not apologize if their work is not psychoanalytically oriented psychotherapy delving into the person's childhood, nor should they feel apologetic about delving into the patient's psychodynamics to deepen their understanding of what causes illness and unhappiness in him.

Several other themes have been dominant in this chapter. First of all, the patient's symptoms should make sense to him and be understood as his reaction to stress. From this understanding can come practical resolutions of his problems. Insofar as possible, this should be a joint process in which both patient and therapist participate. The patient begins to become master of his own destiny.

Probably no part of therapy of the long-term patient is as

important as giving him a sense of mastery (Fenichel, 1946, pp. 13, 460) over his internal drives, his symptoms, and the demands of his environment. From the ability to master and cope with both his internal and external demands comes not only a better adaptation to the world in which he has to live but also a sharp rise in his self-esteem and feelings of self-worth. It is in this context that regression, especially in the form of continued psychotic experiences and ego disintegration, is seen as contraindicated. Such experiences undermine the person's self-confidence and sense of mastery and reinforce his conviction that he is living in a world where he will always be at the mercy of all-powerful forces, both internal and external, which are beyond his control.

It is hoped that this chapter also has underlined the importance of flexibility on the part of the therapist. He must work in the present but be able to delve into the past when necessary. He may at one time serve as a catalyst, while the patient performs the actual decision making, and then in the next hour be equally comfortable as a giver of direct advice or a setter of limits, or both. He must be able to assess when his task is to strengthen the ego and when it is to take sides against the superego. He needs to establish a warm, meaningful relationship without exceeding the patient's tolerance for closeness and intimacy.

In short, he must modify many of the techniques that he learned for working with patients who had quite different problems. But we can accomplish a great deal in psychotherapy with long-term patients. They were formerly relegated to the back wards of state hospitals; they should not be relegated to the backwash of community mental health.

3

Marjorie B. Edelson

Alternative Living Arrangements

Nothing is more revealing in determining whether a long-term patient is truly a part of the community than his housing situation. It can mean the difference between being a member of the community like anybody else or being (to all intents and purposes) institutionalized in a facility that happens to be in an urban or suburban area. To the extent possible, persons who are considered mentally ill should be helped to live in a setting that maximizes their ability to be independent and to participate in community life.

Outside the Mental Health System

In any discussion of living and housing alternatives, it is important to remember that not all mentally ill persons are diagnosed, treated, or receiving services from the established mental health system. Unidentified and unlabeled, some mentally ill persons live in a variety of ways in the community. If they present no danger to themselves or to others, are capable of obtaining the basics of food, clothing, and shelter, and do not desire services, it should be clearly within their rights to remain outside the organized mental health system. California codified these rights in 1969 (Lanterman-Petris-Short Act); other States also have moved to protect the civil rights of this subpopulation from overzealous "casefinding" by professionals and from the overconcern of those in the general public who would like to institutionalize others at the first sign of aberrant behavior.

In earlier times, it was not unusual for an eccentric maiden aunt, a confused grandparent, or an alcoholic uncle to be living within the protection of the family group. Smaller houses, urbanized life-styles, and decreasing importance in our society of relying on the extended family make this phenomenon rarer today. However, in rural areas and within some cultural and ethnic groups, "crazy" behavior still sometimes goes unnamed and is successfully tolerated to a point. Trend data indicate underutilization of mental health services by Asians, blacks, Chicanos and Native Americans. Whether this situation results from cultural and familial tolerance or from a basic distrust of public services is not entirely clear. In any case, many emotionally ill persons are successfully maintained within the family with little or no public intervention.

There also have been times in history when the mentally ill have been revered for their religious visions or because they were thought to be specially touched by the hand of God. (At other times, of course, they have been burned at the stake for demonic possession!) In less sophisticated, usually nonwesternized, societies, the ill person may still be held in awe. But even in our own, familiar world, "special" persons sometimes find a meaningful place in certain religious orders, societies, and sects. Neofundamentalist sects (the youthful so-called Jesus freaks, for instance) may provide a mission in life for the person who preaches and acts upon prophesies and visions which mental health professionals might name delusional. Though philosophically different, some Eastern religious or transcendental meditation groups similarly accept both persons who report experiencing extraordinary inner events and the validity of these events. Other groups that accommodate those who have a different view of reality readily come to mind—for instance, parapsychologists and others who give credence to mystical experiences. There are also religious societies that recognize mental illness as illness but tolerate it and do not exclude the person from the society. This tolerance is not unusual in monastic orders or in the Hutterite communities.

Ambulatory schizophrenics frequently congregate in the so-called counter culture. The pursuit of personal authenticity, particularly by young people, tends to permit acceptance of the psychotic manifestation as original rather than abnormal. That some segments of our society tolerate a wide range of behavioral differences can be verified near any university, in street communities, and in communes. A middle-aged woman recounted a telling incident. She had been invited by young friends to enjoy a sitar performance. Sitting on floor cushions, anticipating the music, the group waited for the performer, who sat huddled in a corner, to begin. He was obviously withdrawn, depressed, and disturbed. The young people gave him support but did not press him. He did not play. The audience was somewhat disappointed, but it was obvious that it did not matter a great deal. When the musician felt better, he would perform. In the meanwhile, his friends would accept him.

A good many of the hermits of earlier times may have been ambulatory schizophrenics. Today, their counterparts may be the skid row isolate (alcohol being a secondary problem), the loner in a slum hotel, the drifter who sleeps under a bridge or on the beach, or the person who builds himself a shack in the wilderness.

The places found in society by the noninstitutionalized, non-identified mentally ill are fascinating to contemplate and worthy of far more space than can be given here. Suffice it to say that living alternatives for some unknown number of persons exist and are successful to at least the same degree as those alternatives provided within the mental health system. The existence of these noninstitutional alternatives should remind us that mental health professionals are not the only resource for the mentally ill. In addition, it is possible to learn something about meeting the needs of the mentally ill from these spontaneous situations. They forcefully remind us that we must truly accept human differences and permit autonomy in the choice of life-style.

Inside the Mental Health System

Long-term patients are not the major consumers of mental health services. If only inpatient treatment is considered, however, the proportion of services provided to long-term patients is appreciably higher than to less severely disabled patients; further, in state hospitals, the chronically ill person has been the major user of services, typically staying a long time, with frequent readmissions. In the economics of mental health services, therefore, this subpopulation is of particular concern, because it claims a disproportionate number of dollars in expensive hospital care. For this reason, and on humanitarian grounds as well, attention now is rightfully focused on alternatives to long-term hospital care for persons who are chronically socially disabled.

Persons who have spent long years in state mental hospitals, or who are part of the population that revolves in and out of local psychiatric inpatient facilities, usually need help in finding a suitable place to live. In many cases, the long-term state hospital patient has no family ties, and the in-and-outer has frequently exhausted his. We say that these patients need to be "placed." An interesting verb, that; it seems to indicate the putting down somewhere of an inanimate object. The word is used throughout this chapter as part of common speech, but it does not embrace the connotation of a nonparticipant sorting of people into predetermined slots.

An important factor in residential treatment is the extent to which the resident is "enveloped" by his housing facility, meaning the extent to which the facility limits the number of life choices the resident is free to make for himself. Put another way, the more caretaking a facility provides, the higher the degree of envelopment.

Examples of high-envelopment resources are hospitals and "therapeutic residential centers." The latter are twenty-four-hour, intensively supervised community facilities that usually are locked; generally, they were established to house, on a relatively long-term basis, severely disabled psychiatric patients who present problems in management. The establishment of these facilities has been a significant development in community mental health and will be described in more detail later. Also included in this category is the "community treatment house," which provides twenty-four-hour intensive treatment in a homelike setting, usually a converted house, on a temporary basis as an alternative to hospitalization.

Mid-range envelopment resources are usually classed as

board and care (residential care) homes. They may be little more than large boardinghouses for a specific population, the mentally ill. Or they may be small, family-type or group homes. Whatever the size, the board and care home provides board, room, nonintensive interaction, and some supervision. The best may have some programmed social-type activities. Although some homes may be therapeutic, their primary purpose is not treatment.

Low-envelopment resources include transitional residences for persons moving toward independent living, satellite or scattered housing, residential hotels, and subsocietal arrangements such as Synanon for drug users and the Fairweather Community Lodge (Fairweather, Sanders, and others, 1969). In the latter model, which Fairweather describes as a sheltered subsociety, a group of long-term patients live and work together with minimal professional supervision and assistance, managing their own business venture and sharing the cooking, housekeeping, and gardening responsibilities.

Still other innovative programs have been developed. Local mental health systems, faced with the responsibility for providing therapeutic community living arrangements for large numbers of returning state hospital patients, have been spurred on not only to improve the places where their charges live but to improvise new programs as well. The Companion Program of the Mental Health Association, Santa Clara County, California, grew out of the recollection that at one time wealthy families paid a companion to look after an eccentric member. In the present context, trained paraprofessionals, available twenty-four hours a day if need be, establish one-to-one relationships with people in crisis in the patient's own milieu. The program has been used very successfully with selected persons in lieu of hospitalization, and at a fraction of the cost. The patient can remain in the community, receiving outpatient treatment, because there is a supportive, nurturing person with him during the period when he feels immobilized and helpless. Similar but far less intensive are companion programs staffed by volunteers (see Chapter Seven) and homemaker services that provide concrete help and role models for the patient with a family.

Would fewer persons require out-of-home placement at all if families could count on support and respite? Undoubtedly. Such has been the experience with developmentally disabled and schizophrenic children. Although the families of older, long-term schizophrenics perhaps are weary of coping with the patient's behavior, or perhaps have a different psychological set, many families usually are willing to try the patient at home if the responsibility is not constant. Just as members of any family need experiences separate and away from the family group, so do families with a mentally ill member. If freedom from constant responsibility is not planned for, it may be obtained by rehospitalization of the patient. Halfway houses or satellite living programs can provide respite care and should recognize the importance of this function, perhaps even to the extent of designating one or more beds for this purpose. Another way to offer respite is illustrated in sponsoring family or crisis homes programs, which offer temporary out-of-home placement to individual patients. The purpose is to provide a resource for an individual in turmoil so that he and his family experience some respite from each other while problems are resolved. In such a situation, the sponsoring family also serves as a role model for the dysfunctional family.

The Missouri Foster Community Program. An innovative community living program from the standpoint of mobilization of community involvement is Missouri's Foster Community Program (Keskiner, Zalcman, and others, 1972). Patterning their state hospital placement program after the Gheel Colony in Belgium, the Missouri Institute of Psychiatry and the St. Louis State Hospital have, since 1968, been working successfully with two small (population under three thousand) rural towns to provide foster homes and a supportive environment for a group of long-term patients who have completed an extensive in-hospital resocialization program. Local leadership and popular support were enlisted to implement a community-wide placement and socialization program. All efforts were geared toward involving citizens in integrating the patients into community life, even to the extent of establishing a formal citizens' organization as a nonprofit corporation. This corporation directs and operates the program in conjunction with project staff. The corporation's board of directors recruits placement resources, organizes special social events, and publicizes and promotes the program by using local newspapers and giving talks before local groups.

Crucial to the success of this project is careful preparation of townspeople through a process of mental health education, so that the presence and participation of patients in the community is accepted. Social contacts between patients and townspeople enhance the learning process. After the groundwork has been laid, patients (limited in number to avoid community saturation) move into the homes of foster families or into shared apartments. The community corporation approves placement plans and is directly involved in continuing care of the patients along with the hospital project staff. Intensive community involvement and a goal of assimilation are the keys to this program.

Once the initial community organization has been accomplished and the program established, such a project is inexpensive. In the Missouri program, each town has fifteen patients and is assigned a half-time professional who lives in the town. There is also administrative backup at the head office in St. Louis. When the patients encounter a problem, townspeople frequently provide the assistance that, in other community placements, is given by professionals. The function of a foster community for former state hospital patients has been incorporated into the identity of each town; even though the federal grant has long since ended and the professionals who instituted the program have departed, the interest of the townspeople in their foster citizens and the concept itself remains strong.

"Patients who move into the foster community are regarded as new residents and they are encouraged to enter into community life by joining churches or social organizations and registering to vote. They do their banking, shopping, and other household business in the community and they may participate in community activities as well as any other citizen. Although employment is not a requirement, those who are interested are encouraged and assisted in finding a job. Some have obtained full-time jobs in local businesses or part-time jobs with families, while others have made use of community resources such as sheltered workshops or craft groups" (Keskiner and Zalcman, 1974, p. 423).

Satellite Housing. Perhaps the most promising concept for housing large numbers of long-term patients is satellite housing. Satellite housing may be apartments, duplexes, or small, single-family dwellings. The housing is leased by the residents or the mother agency or coleased by both. Here patients live in small groups of two to five, without live-in staff but with some professional supervision. No other therapeutic housing program comes closer to helping long-term patients live normal lives in the community. Although many of these programs have begun as resources for graduates of more structured programs, such as halfway houses, the feasibility of direct placement into satellite housing has been demonstrated (Sandall, Hawley, and Gordon, 1975). An increasing number of patients, referred from hospitals and psychiatric agencies, are now placed in a satellite situation directly, with overall good results. This arrangement has several significant advantages. It means less use of halfway houses with their expensive around-the-clock staffing and the other costs inherent in setting up and running a small institution. But even more important, the patient has only one adjustment to make—from the hospital subculture to satellite housing. With the halfway house interposed, there are two separate cultural adaptations—first the transition from the hospital to the halfway house and then, after adaptation to the halfway house subculture, the move to satellite housing.

The existence of a large number of community apartments increases the possibility that roommates can be matched in terms of age, personality, interests, and level of functioning. Shopping, cooking, and housework are shared, and residents have a responsibility for paying the rent (either to the landlord directly or to the agency). Staff members assigned to satellite housing programs are available as needed for guidance and counseling, both individual and group, and are also available on a twenty-four-hour, on-call basis for emergencies. In the satellite program in San Mateo County, California, residents of three or four apartments form a stable group for regular meetings, both with staff and at times without staff present. These group meetings are hosted by the residents within their own housing units on a rotating basis.

Satellite housing programs have a high-expectation philosophy in the sense that residents are expected to have a meaningful daytime activity outside of the house in addition to helping with the chores at home. It is important that this requirement be flexible. Many residents comfortably spend their days in short-term day treatment centers, vocational rehabilitation programs, or competitive employment. But some persons, otherwise entirely suited for satellite housing, will only be able to handle a friendship center (see Chapter Seven) a few hours a week. Still others may find the requirement for an outside activity of any kind more than they can handle, at least at first. Hasty judgments to shift such patients to lower-expectation–higher-envelopment programs should not be made. A satellite unit can be organized on a family model, in which some residents have an outside daytime activity and others remain at home, perhaps taking responsibility for cooking the meals and cleaning the house. For many persons, simply living in the unstructured setting of a satellite apartment, with only a few responsibilities, is the limit of these persons' capabilities at that particular time; asking only this much of such persons is for them high expectations.

Ideally, staff intervention also will be flexible. The fragile, fearful resident with a limited anxiety tolerance needs more staff support than other residents. A period of close contact between staff and a resident, his apartment mates, and his therapist may often head off a crisis that might lead to rehospitalization. Occasionally, such a resident will need to be removed from his apartment and placed for a brief period in a halfway house or community treatment house (see below) or a local hospital.

There should be flexibility to decrease services as well as to increase them. Some satellite residents can stabilize at a level where staff intervention or supervision is no longer needed, except on an occasional basis. At this point, the residents have made a normal adjustment to the community, and the goal of complete integration has been met.

Two High-Envelopment Facilities. The development of new high-envelopment community facilities has been an important event in community mental health. But this development has been so rapid that a new classification and nomenclature has not grown up to keep pace with it. Consequently, there is considerable confusion not only about what to call these facilities but also about the important concepts that underlie them. The classification presented here uses two general categories, the community treatment house and the therapeutic residential center. The distinctions between them are based on the type of building used, the amount of structure provided in terms of security, locked doors, and intensive supervision, and the purpose of the facility. The last distinction is especially confusing inasmuch as there is considerable overlap. For instance, both facilities are used to significantly shorten the length of hospitalization by taking patients after a brief evaluation and after initial stabilization on an acute inpatient service.

More and more long-term patients, in crisis and acutely psychotic, are receiving relatively brief high-envelopment care in these alternatives to high-cost hospital wards. The "community treatment house" (our name) is a facility that incorporates some of the elements of hospital treatment (twenty-four-hour supervision, high staff ratio, and intensive treatment) into a more homelike, community setting, generally in a converted house (Goveia and Tutko, 1969). In some instances, the community treatment house is used in lieu of hospitalization, in which case it is often called a precare or crisis house. In others, it follows a brief diagnostic period in a hospital, and in still others, it is used for both purposes. Having a relatively high staff-patient ratio, it offers intensive patient-staff interaction but does not have such security features as locked doors, unbreakable glass windows, and seclusion rooms; patients needing this kind of facility are not treated here. Developed as a lower-cost alternative to psychiatric hospitalization (usually less than half the per diem cost), these programs are proving their effectiveness in stabilizing many acutely ill persons in a homelike environment and preparing them for the transition either to family life or to a less intensive residential program. Here patients may get therapeutic benefits from cooperative housework, cooking, and planning everyday activities, as well as a structured milieu, group and individual treatment, and regulated medication, without the built-in encouragement of dependency, infantilization, and infirmity found in even a progressive hospital.

The author recognizes the importance of brief hospital care for the long-term patient when there are medical considerations, such as the need to adjust medication because of cardiovascular problems or to stabilize a patient whose behavior is grossly out of control. Though this chapter is not primarily concerned with acute hospital treatment and its alternatives, placement as soon as possible in high-envelopment, nonhospital, residential treatment centers is extremely important because it minimizes institutionalization and isolation from the community, even at a time when twenty-four-hour super-vision is required.

Another model of high-envelopment residential treatment, but usually on a longer term basis, is what Atkinson (1975) calls the "therapeutic residential center" (often referred to as an inter-mediate facility, a "psychiatric skilled nursing facility," or an "L facility" in California)'. Some facilities are built expressly for the purpose of treating chronically disabled psychiatric patients. Others are converted convalescent hospitals, but are a far cry from the convalescent hospital or nursing home for the aged. These facilities accommodate thirty to one hundred patients and usually have locked doors and other security features. They provide twenty-four-hour care, over long periods of time if necessary, for severely dis-turbed and difficult to manage patients. The increasing use of these facilities for younger patients reflects a growing recognition that many persons can be kept out of state hospitals only if there is a structured and intensively supervised facility available as an alterna-tive. These therapeutic residential centers usually are long-term, but not terminal. Smaller than state hospitals, they can provide more intensive interaction and individual attention. The patient is not removed from his home community, and the program uses com-munity resources. The patient is expected to succeed, in time, in a more independent living situation.

Like the community treatment house, the therapeutic resi-dential center serves the acutely ill after a brief period in a hospital. It also serves as an alternative to hospitalization in a situation where a patient has become unmanageable or persona non grata in a board and care home. Frequently, the security of the therapeu-tic residential center, a few weeks of asylum there, and some work by his aftercare team in finding a more suitable board and care home, or getting him back on his medications, or resolving a prob-lem in his vocational activity or in his personal life, are enough to prevent a hospitalization.

In California, we have seen the side-by-side development of two different but congruent ways of funding long-term residential treatment and rehabilitation in these community therapeutic resi-dential centers. For facilities that meet specified rehabilitative ob-jectives of staffing and treatment, Medicaid has been able to pay a cost differential for this treatment. These programs are geared to the long-term patient who in times past would have been considered custodial by a convalscent hospital or a state institution. Usually by means of behavior modification techniques, such as rewarding socially acceptable behavior with additional privileges, these centers work to eliminate behavior that is unacceptable at less structured levels of care and to reinforce positive social behavior. Many patients are enabled to move from therapeutic residential centers to board and care homes, to their own families, and, more rarely, to independent living.

The second method of funding provides for even more intensive treatment. In this instance, a county mental health program provides a "psychiatric patch" of mental health staff to work within the facility. This staff supplements the basic supervised living program. The program may include group and individual treatment, recreation and occupational therapy, and projects geared to increase the chronic patient's skills in daily living. An all-out effort is mounted to treat and rehabilitate the long-term patient so that he can move out of custodial care and truly into the community.

For purposes of contrast, let us review the other end of the envelopment spectrum, satellite housing (which has been discussed in an earlier section). Since, for the most part, the residents have the potential for greater independence and the milieu is geared toward fostering that independence, therapy is provided outside the home. Residents usually share in the everyday household chores, do their own laundry, buy their own clothes, and manage their own medications and therapy appointments. In-house social problems are handled directly, through house government meetings, residents and the staff. Staff are usually mental health workers who have access to psychiatric consultation. On-the-spot counseling, rather than formal therapy, tends to be the mode of in-house treatment, along with therapeutic community activities. House activities are planned for evenings and weekends, as the resident is usually gone during the daytime hours.

Residential Care Homes. The residential care (board and care) home, by far the largest placement resource for long-term schizophrenics, traditionally has been the least therapeutic milieu.

All too often it has been a place where a well-meaning proprietor has cared for patients for profit and for psychological satisfaction, but without proper guidance. For instance, the operator may need to continue the parental role in order to feel useful. Such motivation is neither good nor bad in and of itself. But the operator must encourage residents to realize their full potential by utilizing treatment and rehabilitation resources outside the home. The operator would then be taking a mature parental attitude that provides a more meaningful and positive living alternative for the patient. A clearcut mandate for operators to encourage and facilitate rehabilitation is essential in avoiding situations such as that described by Silberstein (1969, p. 2): "Caretakers were quite maternal, met the physical needs of their guests, and related to them as they would to young children." Field workers are quite familiar with situations in which residents, who have assumed a docile and passive role, show ability to manage a household quite competently in emergencies such as an unexpected hospitalization of the operator.

One of the most important support services that mental health programs can provide is consultation, education, and training for facility operators as a means of fostering attitudes productive of patient growth. Chapter Four will describe this process in some detail. In communities where there is active consultation and training, residential care operators tend to see themselves as professionals. Indeed, in one community, people in this business are called "community care administrators." This title changes the psychological attitude not only of the administrators, but of the residents and referring professionals as well.

Reorienting residential care home administrators is, of course, only part of the process of making these facilities more therapeutic. Resources outside the home, such as sheltered workshops, vocational rehabilitation counseling, day treatment programs, and outpatient treatment, are necessary. Also needed are social rehabilitation programs that help the long-term patient learn how to utilize leisure time and acquire social competence (see Chapter Seven). These programs are an important addendum to the living situation, enriching the resident's life in exactly the same way as a social life away from home provides new dimensions for the normal individual. Without adequate treatment and rehabilitation programs, community living may be as institutionalizing as the worst state hospital.

Within the facility itself, on-the-spot, practical counseling should be available from the administrator and her helpers. Social functions should be promoted, and the administrator should help to organize activities. The introduction of volunteers from outside the home is often a help in this area. In San Jose, California, college students are active in the board and care community on a regular and innovative basis. Their program, called "Community of Communities," is described in Chapter Seven.

In any kind of residential setting for the mentally ill, the atmosphere should be conducive to promoting the residents' coping abilities and self-esteem. Participation in running the household, both chores and decision-making, is an important educational process as long as it is not exploitive or pursued begrudgingly by the administrator. Patients should be encouraged to attend to their personal hygiene needs themselves. Cooperative, nonabrasive social interaction should be promoted. As residents improve, expectations should be raised and the amount of independent activity enlarged. Although some chronically disabled persons may never progress beyond board and care living, opportunities for growth and movement toward less enveloping situations should be fostered.

Support to facility administrators (and to families, for that matter) in the form of crisis services, preferably mobile, should be readily available. The more difficult patients coming out of the state hospitals usually can be placed and maintained if the residential care administrator (or the family) knows that help is immediately available should difficult or unmanageable behavior occur. An immediate determination of the problems can be an educational experience for an administrator and a therapeutic one for the patient. Moreover, it can often interrupt the pattern of failure and continued undermining of the patient's sense of mastery that is inevitable when the patient is relocated or hospitalized at every crisis point.

Toward a Therapeutic Milieu

It is hoped that all residential programs for the mentally disabled attempt to provide a therapeutic milieu. What are the basic features of a therapeutic milieu? A few are a climate of emotional support; clarity of behavioral expectations in all communications between staff and residents; autonomy in as great a degree as the resident can handle; a practical orientation toward helping the resident deal with the problems of everyday living; and expectations based on a realistic assessment of the resident's capabilities.

Direct treatment in the facility usually decreases with decreasing envelopment. High-envelopment programs such as acute inpatient units have intensive on-ward treatment programs. Residents in facilities with the lowest degree of envelopment are expected to arrange for whatever treatment is indicated outside the living facility. This policy is in line with the principle of encouraging the psychiatric patient to make as many of his own decisions as possible (selecting the kind and place of treatment) and the principle of normalization (going outside the residence for treatment services in the way any other member of the population does).

We must recognize that some patients are able to handle only the least demanding of the community residential programs just described. Extreme negativism, hyperactivity, and need for external controls may make a structured, locked setting necessary. Assaultiveness, firesetting, and unmanageable self-destructiveness may also require a maximum security facility such as a state hospital (Lamb and Goertzel, 1972).

Matching Patients and Facilities

Choice of the community placement facility is generally determined by the level at which the patient is able to function. For instance, residential treatment centers are designed for patients who require twenty-four-hour care and supervision. Patients placed in residential care (board and care) homes must have a fair capacity to manage their physical needs independently, such as bathing, dressing, and taking medication. Halfway house residents must evidence even more capacity for handling responsibility and must indicate a potential for work or activity outside of the residence. Careful assessment of the patient's functioning is essential in making placement plans. The decision should be guided by the principle that the degree of envelopment should be the least possible; treatment should be geared toward moving the patient downward on the envelopment scale.

The patient's treatment needs are also determinants in choice of placement. Does the patient need some time in a locked community facility to regain a sense of security? Does he need a large board and care situation, where a need for distance will not be violated? Or does he need a family setting for closeness? Is a transitional residence with greater freedom indicated by his level of independence? Ideally, by the time the patient is ready to leave an inpatient unit, a careful aftercare plan has been developed with him that includes recommendations for type of living situation, treatment program, medications, and social rehabilitation. The aftercare plan is the roadmap in finding appropriate resources. Although such a plan is the ideal, it is naïve to think it is the rule. With the current de-emphasis on hospital care, patients tend to move so rapidly through local inpatient units that there is little opportunity for refined planning. Although state hospital stays are longer and discharge planning more leisurely, the current trend is for long-term patients to be treated briefly for acute exacerbations of illness in local hospitals, where the pattern of institutional dependency will not be reinforced.

What, then, is the capability for aftercare planning for the short-stay patient? Probably not enough. Although short stays have led to enriched staffing to provide intensive brief therapy on hospital wards, this staffing is not necessarily extended to discharge planning. One answer to this problem has been the development of extra-hospital mental health teams specifically charged with the responsibility for planning and implementing continuing care. This specialized staff, usually social workers, nurses, and mental health workers, know the community's resources and frequently have had prior experience with the particular long-term patient. The aftercare staff participate in the design of the patient's discharge plan, working with the hospital staff and the patient while he is still hospitalized. Postdischarge follow-up to see that the patient has actually followed through with his aftercare plan and has not "fallen between the cracks" while moving from hospital to community is another key role of the aftercare staff.

The patient must be consulted about where he would prefer to live and what the available choices are. Although the staff of necessity defines the patient's condition and recommends a treatment plan, if the plan is completed without the participation of the central figure, it may be a disaster. Not only does ignoring the patient diminish the integrity of a person whose self-concept is already damaged, but it is also pragmatically unsound. The patient frequently knows better than the staff where he is and what he needs.

In selecting his posthospital home, the patient should be aware of the expectations the facility administrator has of him. Likewise, the administrator's obligations to the patient should be made explicit. Perhaps there should be a contract, signed by both administrator and resident, spelling out the rights, duties, and expectations of both and the circumstances under which the relationship may be terminated by either.

Another placement determinant is personality—that of the person to be placed and those of the facility administrator, staff, and other residents living in the facility. An active, independent patient will be stifled in a home with a mothering caretaker and passive, dependent fellow residents. On the other hand, a facility administrator with a need to see quick success will not tolerate a regressed or passive-aggressive person very well. Matching patient and facility requires delicate balancing, a just right mixing of ingredients so that there are enough challenges to provoke growth while at the same time the facility and the patient are relatively comfortable with each other. The matching process is not static either. Aftercare staff must be alert to changing needs as the patient progresses, or to changes in the atmosphere of a facility that may necessitate an adjustment.

Ideally, then, the matching process is tridimensional in character, determined by the level at which the patient can function, the patient's treatment needs, and the patient's personality in relation to the personalities of staff and other residents at a given facility. Frequently, however, the crucial factor is a fourth determinant—availability.

The problem of availability may be one of timing (no appropriate vacancy at the exact time it is needed), or it may result from an inadequate range of community resources. Perhaps the placement of choice is a halfway house, but the local community has none. Choices may be limited, therefore, to keeping the patient longer in an acute hospital, trying the patient in a residence club or satellite apartment for which he is not quite ready, placing him in a poor-quality board and care home where he may regress, or placing him in an appropriate facility away from the home community. This quite common example points up the need for a wide spectrum of living resources in a compact geographic area. This range of facilities is not always practical in large, sprawling, sparsely populated areas, however. In this instance, resource planning may have to be on a regional rather than a community basis.

Economic pressure on facility administrators to fill beds is very real. If the choice of facilities is large, the vacancy factor may be high, as it will be if patients are actively encouraged to consider supervised housing as transitional and temporary. If the time ever arrives when there is an adequate range and number of facilities, it may be necessary to consider the temporary public subsidy of vacant beds so that facility administrators do not discourage progress in order to keep their beds full. A precedent already is provided by foster home programs for children in which nonfilled beds are paid for in order to ensure vacancies for emergency situations.

The Mental Health Ghetto

With the shift from state hospital to community treatment, we have experienced the phenomenon of the "mental health ghetto." In Chicago, mentally disabled persons are living in large, run-down old residential hotels in transitional neighborhoods. Some of these hotels house over five hundred ex-patients, and the atmosphere is depressing. San Jose, California, is another example. At this time, it is estimated that about eleven hundred former hospital patients (plus another six hundred drug abusers and alcoholics) live in over one hundred board and care homes in a fifteen-square-block area in downtown San Jose (Moltzen, 1975, p. 3). This situation was not planned, but grew out of coincidental events. At the same time that emphasis on the community placement of patients from a nearby state hospital was increasing, the local university was loosening restrictions on off-campus housing for students. Thus, at the time that demand for patient homes was growing, the large, "approved" student boardinghouses were being emptied. Private enterprise did the rest.

There are many other communities near state hospitals where a board and care industry has grown up around the hospital. This concentration of the chronically disabled hardly fits the concept of integrating the mentally ill into the mainstream of community life. The best that can be said for such a de facto segregation is that there are some advantages for providing aftercare services in a centralized area, mostly within walking distance of the homes.

Local zoning ordinances, requirements for use permits, or interpretations of other ordinances have been used to keep residential facilities out of some communities and some neighborhoods. The needs of the people who will live in such facilities often have less influence than the question of where there will be the least neighborhood opposition. Consequently, facilities tend to be concentrated in certain quasi-commercial areas. It must be noted here that restrictive ordinances are but responses to the fears and concerns of citizens. These concerns usually focus on two issues—danger to life and diminished property values.

It is not the purpose of this chapter to consider in depth the potential dangerousness of mental patients to the community; studies support both sides of the question. The incidence of crime among long-term schizophrenics, however, is probably lower than among the general population. For the police, the more important problem appears to be the burden of dealing with psychiatric patients who are lost and wandering around the neighborhood, or, less frequently, exhibiting bizarre behavior (Atkinson, 1975). For instance, early in 1975, the San Jose Police Department undertook a study to measure the amount of time police officers spend handling problems in the large board and care community referred to above. They found that almost all police contacts, and there were only twenty-nine in the forty-eight days studied, were the result of disturbance of the peace complaints, missing persons reports, and requests for police assistance. No crimes of violence were committed by the residents (*Mental Health Association of Santa Clara County Newsletter*, 1975). It is hoped that the trend of releasing most long-term patients to the community will continue regardless of their degree of regression or even bizarreness. But in our enthusiasm, we must not lose sight of the need to screen persons with a history of violence carefully. If the patient still presents a potential for violence, we have an obligation to protect the community—and the patient —by placing him in a setting, locked if necessary, that will provide him with the structure he needs.

Langsley and Barter (1975, p. 166) wrote: "We must also face the fact that community treatment will probably increase the presence of persons who constitute nuisances rather than real threats to the public safety. In the past, mental hospitals (asylums) were used to remove this type of person from society. In part, this was a consequence of public fears about mental illness. . . . The suggestion that we simply lock up psychotics until they are 'cured' or until we can guarantee a high level of adaptation to the community is simplistic. It is also expensive in terms of human suffering and economic cost."

The general public is very concerned about the effect of the presence of disabled persons on neighborhood property values. However, an extensive study in Green Bay, Wisconsin (Knowles and Baba, 1973), demonstrated that such fears are not justified; property values did not go down.

Another factor that leads to concentration of residential facilities in commercial, transitional, or run-down neighborhoods is property costs. Since most facilities are established as a business venture, proprietors will seek out areas where housing is cheap in order to increase their profit margins. Moreover, residents, often supported by the welfare system, cannot afford to pay high room-and-board rates.

An important factor leading to the development of mental health ghettos is the tendency of communities physically to exclude the mentally ill. Although state hospitals traditionally have been used for physical exclusion, trends in community mental health and changes in state laws, as for instance in California (Urmer, 1975), have made this recourse of commitment and prolonged involuntary confinement difficult. Society is able to maintain distance nonetheless by formal mechanisms such as increased penal commitments, zoning laws, and other city ordinances and by informal mechanisms such as neighborhood pressures and bureaucratic maneuvering (Aviram and Segal, 1973). In any case, physical inclusion in a community is not enough; social inclusion, a willingness among community members to allow a decrease in their social distance from the mentally ill living among them, is necessary for true integration.

Other Problem Areas

The publicly supported resident of a community facility (the great majority) is the recipient of aid from a partnership of two systems—welfare and community mental health. Room-and-board costs are usually supported out of the resident's Supplemental Security Income (SSI; formerly Aid to the Disabled), while community mental health pays for treatment costs. The lines of separation in a system that relies heavily on "milieu" treatment are indistinct and often artificial. In California, accounting headaches and difficulties in matching the rapid pace of placement with the ponderous SSI system have led to the formulation of a "life support" policy that allows the state mental health funding mechanism to pick up as necessary total costs (treatment plus board and room) in facilities that are truly residential treatment centers (not board and care homes). This solution is doubled-edged in that it uses scarce mental health treatment dollars to pay board and room costs for which another governmental system (welfare) has responsibility.

A second funding-related problem has to do with the impact on programs of revenue sources. Most private insurance and Medicaid will pay the full costs of care in high-envelopment programs such as hospitals and therapeutic residential centers. In other types of residential treatment, however, it is likely that only visits by a psychiatrist and not the total cost of the program will be reimbursed. Thus, higher envelopment than is necessary for the patient's recovery is encouraged.

The use of rate structures to reward rehabilitative programs is also an important issue. In California, increased Medicaid rates are now paid to therapeutic residential centers that have approved "rehabilitation" or "subacute" treatment programs. In order to bring to fruition the expectation that all residential care should be therapeutic, it is necessary to carry the principle of increased payment for increased programming throughout the total range of community facilities.

Another problem area is licensing. Licensing is primarily intended to protect the disabled person who is cared for in a facility. The inherent problem is that since licensing regulations cover a broad range of facilities, programming may inadvertently be restricted by licensing requirements. A community treatment facility planned for use as a substitute for lengthy hospital care may find it impossible to conform to construction, seismic-safety, and fire-safety regulations unless it is in a hospitallike structure that is both expensive and countertherapeutic in terms of providing a normalized living situation. Although licensing is desirable in principle, regulations should clearly differentiate children and the physically disabled from those mentally ill persons who do not need the same degree of physical protection. Also, those who administer licensing regulations should have enough flexibility to give program needs at least as high a priority as physical structure requirements.

Conclusions

Living alternatives for the long-term psychiatric patient requiring out-of-home placement should cover a whole spectrum, ranging from highest-envelopment systems down to minimal professional contacts. A great deal of innovation is taking place in regard both to alternatives to hospital care and the provision of more normal living experiences for the posthospital patient. The Missouri Foster Community Program is an interesting experiment in total community involvement. But perhaps the most encouraging opportunities for integrating large numbers of chronically disabled persons into the community are satellite housing programs, where the mentally ill may live normal lives with the help of professional support and some supervision.

A therapeutic milieu is essential in all residential resources. In-house treatment programs usually decrease as the patient achieves independence, but a climate must always be maintained in which the patient's gradual movement to lower-envelopment placements is encouraged. Expectations realistically geared to the abilities of the patient at any given time allow the development of his full potential.

Support systems apart from the residence are essential. For the patient, these may be outpatient treatment programs, medication clinics, vocational rehabilitation programs, day treatment centers, and activity groups. For the facility administrator (as for the family), consultation, crisis intervention, and respite services are crucial. Available resources in the form of volunteers and public services outside of mental health (libraries, recreation departments, schools, and the like) are beginning to be tapped to a considerable extent.

Finally, the tendency to segregate mental patients into circumscribed residential areas, because of cost, public resistance, and sometimes apathy on the part of mental health professionals, must be overcome if long-term patients are to be truly a part of the community.

Richard A. Shadoan

4

Making Board and Care Homes Therapeutic

Community mental health centers are well into their second decade of operation and have achieved considerable success in providing immediate, community-oriented treatment. However, the persons treated generally have been people who know how to take advantage of the opportunity or who have such acute illnesses that the community responds by taking them to a caregiving facility. The long-term, chronically mentally ill have not been able or willing to use what is offered. Moreover, the original Community Mental Health Centers Act of 1963 was not really geared to the clinical needs of the long-term patient. The now familiar five essential services (inpatient, outpatient, emergency, day care, and consultation) neglect this type of patient. Many mental health professionals and the Congress are now aware of this neglect. The Community Mental Health Center Amendments of 1975 add seven new essential services, among them community living programs that could offer effective alternatives to institutional care for the severely handicapped chronic patient.

In addition to legislation, powerful forces at work in the legal system under the rubric "right to treatment" may help the long-term patient survive in the community. The number of advocates of the disabled psychiatric patient's right to treatment in the community is growing, and they have taken this matter to the courts. Thus, legislation, the courts, some mental health workers, and to some extent patients and the general public, are all demanding that community programs now focus on the clinical needs of the chronically ill.

Probably no area of the community mental health movement has drawn more severe criticism than the community living programs. Some critics call for increasing the number of halfway houses, but when the number required for tens of thousands of patients is contemplated, the task becomes monumental. Furthermore, halfway houses traditionally have been afflicted with the YAWVIS syndrome, an acronym referring to a preference for young, adult, white, verbal, intelligent, sophisticated patients. Also, halfway houses generally limit stays to six months to a year and usually require that the resident have reached a level of functioning and motivation sufficient for involvement in a daytime program outside the house. Obviously, the halfway house excludes most members of the very group we are trying to reach.

Another approach that has been employed during the last decade is placement of the chronically mentally ill in boarding homes, foster homes, and the like. But the hope that this type of home would provide a more normal, socially balanced environment than that offered by a hospital has not been realized. A study of patients in fifty-eight foster homes in Quebec, Ontario, and New Brunswick supports the clinical impression that such programs do not improve social skills (Murphy, Engelsmann, and Toheng-LaRoche, in press). In terms of clinical symptoms, the home-placement group improved almost as much as did the group that remained in the hospital. But, in social involvement and participation, the home placement group showed less improvement. There was a shift toward passivity and social stagnation rather than toward social reinvolvement.

What is lacking is a program of treatment that comes to the resident and develops the home into a twenty-four-hour therapeutic community. What is needed is a home environment that exerts major therapeutic leverage on the resident to change his self-image from hopeless to hopeful, helpless to helpful, worthless to worthwhile, dependent to independent. The thesis of this chapter is that residential care facilities (formerly called "board and care homes") offer an opportunity to create high-quality therapeutic living situations for tens of thousands of long-term patients.

A Personal Note

For me, involvement with residential care facilities came about through a patient I was seeing in outpatient psychotherapy.

A forty-seven-year-old woman, with a long history of repeated hospitalizations, was living in a residential care facility and began to decompensate over a period of several weeks. She became increasingly disruptive, and finally she physically attacked another patient in my waiting room. As it was impossible to continue seeing her at my office, I asked the administrator of the residential care facility whether I could see the patient there. The administrator readily agreed and asked that we discuss how to deal with the patient, who was causing a great deal of turmoil in the house—using abusive language, attacking other residents, cutting the cord to the television. The other fourteen residents were angry and wanted her to leave immediately. I suggested weekly meetings, which all the residents would attend, to discuss the problem. Although the meetings did not solve the specific problem, they did provide a channel for examining and expressing feelings, which seemed to reduce tensions.

It was eventually decided to transfer my patient to another facility, but my being able to continue seeing her when she was too disturbed to come to my office had been extremely important for her eventual stabilization. She is now living independently, going to school part-time, and working at a volunteer job. Also, it was important for the other residents to be able to discuss their anger and, what proved even more important, their feelings of guilt over wanting my patient to leave.

Some of the issues revolved around such concerns as, If another resident began to decompensate, would the rest of the group be helpful or rejecting? How can the residents help one another during a crisis? If another resident decompensates and has to leave, what is the appropriate responsibility each resident should assume?

The administrator felt our meetings were so helpful during this crisis that she asked me to continue them. The residents were ambivalent. Some felt they were being disloyal to their own psychiatrists if they attended the house meeting. Several psychiatrists were wary that I might be attempting to take their patients away, but I was able to correct any misunderstandings by calling each psychiatrist and explaining the purpose of the meetings. Other residents were fearful of sharing feelings in a group or of being criticized. After several weeks' discussion and strong encouragement from the administrator and from the bolder residents, it was agreed to give the meetings a two-month trial. One of the residents was elected chairperson and another secretary. The weekly meetings have now continued for over two years.

Creating a Therapeutic Community Milieu

A major task in making residential care facilities therapeutic is development of a high-expectation atmosphere in the home. All too often in the past, merely helping persons survive was considered adequate care (the "warehousing" concept). But the impact of psychotherapy, day programs, and vocational training will be greatly lessened if the resident returns to a home reflecting an atmosphere of helplessness, social isolation, and timelessness. In addition, it is in the home that the activities of daily life needed for achieving some measure of independent living can be learned.

One important avenue for creating a therapeutic community in the home is the weekly house meeting, which helps to develop a spirit of cohesiveness. It also provides a forum for discussion of issues and conflicts, so that the individual has an alternative to withdrawal, resignation, or acting out. Mental health workers in residential care facilities need to be well grounded in theories of group processes in order to understand and respond to the unconscious processes that take place in group living. (The conferences on group processes sponsored by the A. K. Rice Institute are an excellent educational resource in this area.)

One of the most significant covert processes that pervades the residential care home is the denial by residents of the importance of events that take place in their own lives or in the lives of other residents. Conflicts that arise among the residents or between the residents and the administrator often are denied. Issues such as integrating a new resident, dealing with feelings of loss when a resident leaves, handling a crisis in the home or in a resident's life, or coping with the death of a resident are usually handled by a mask of indifference.

Case illustration: A sixty-five-year-old woman who had been in a residential care home for ten years died of a heart attack. The next day, during the house meeting, her death was mentioned, as was the fact that arrangements concerning her burial were uncertain. The discussion moved on to typical business—an upcoming outing, noise the preceding night, and unclean toilets—but was conducted in a rather agitated manner. It was pointed out that the group seemed to be avoiding some things. This assertion was strongly denied, and trivial conversation ensued.

Finally, the mental health worker suggested that the group was avoiding the painful subject of the death of one of the residents. Very tentatively at first, almost as if they were afraid to admit that they did care, the group began sharing their feelings about the deceased resident. It soon became clear that although this resident had been older and more quiet than the others in the home, most of them had developed a special relationship with her. The meeting seemed to overcome the fear of showing interest and caring. Over the next few days, the residents experienced some meaningful feelings of mourning, made arrangements for the funeral, and then attended it.

Another way of creating a therapeutic community is by having residents assume important positions in the management of the home. Those residents and facility administrators who view the home as a place responsible for giving board and care rather than as a community that expects active participation and learning must be reeducated. Many residents fear taking on responsibilities because they might fail or be criticized.

Case illustration: One home had a housekeeper one day a week to vacuum, dust, wash floors, change linen, iron, and the like.

For several weeks, at the house meetings, the residents discussed the possibility of their assuming these duties. Some residents maintained that they were paying to be taken care of and didn't want to be involved in cleaning a home. Others felt that they lacked appropriate skills. A few of the men said this was women's work. Still others said they had worked in hospitals under the guise of therapy and felt that the hospital had taken advantage of them.

These and other issues were discussed, along with some reality testing. "No, you are not in this home for the purpose of sitting around passively paying to be taken care of. You are paying to live here in order to learn skills of daily living and socialization. Yes, some of you may have been forced to work under the guise of therapy. Yes, you may have lost skills, but you can relearn them." It was finally decided to divide the housekeeper's work into eight jobs, with eight residents each taking one job. As there were more than eight residents, several additional jobs were offered—helping with meals, washing dishes, handling the mail. For a brief period the housekeeper supervised the residents' work. But it soon became apparent that this supervision was not necessary. From the money saved by dispensing with a housekeeper, the administrator was able to pay the residents a dollar an hour. More importantly, the residents began seeing the home as "our" home instead of "their" home and took a much more active interest in its successful management.

With such an orientation, a different primary task emerges for the administrators. For years they have been called "caretakers" and have seen taking care of the residents as their principal duty. But the emphasis should be on teaching residents how to care for themselves; that is, administrators should be "care teachers."

Case illustration: One administrator was very proud that her residents never missed a doctor's appointment. Closer questioning revealed that she personally escorted them to the appointments. A meeting was held with the physician, the conservator, the mental health worker, and the administrator. Discussion centered on the fact that, even though it was important for the residents not to miss their appointments, personal escorting was giving the residents the explicit message that they were not capable of keeping appointments. In the case of one resident, the central issue of his psychotherapy was his difficulty in assuming responsibility for himself. Much of the insight he was gaining in this conflictive area was being negated by his being transported to and from appointments. With some apprehension, it was decided the issue should be discussed with the residents. This discussion led to a mutual agreement that they would be taught how to reach their physicians by public transportation. After initial anxiety, the residents were pleased to have been given this responsibility.

Not only must the home create its own atmosphere of independence, but also forces outside the home must encourage the resident to view himself as potentially self-sufficient.

Case illustration: At one home, medication for the residents was delivered. The residents seemed quite content with this arrangement, stating that the pharmacist encouraged the residents to have their medication delivered. The pharmacist was invited to the next house meeting. He explained that there might be a fifteen-to-twenty-minute wait while prescriptions were being filled. He felt that "these people" might have difficulty tolerating a delay and that their behavior in the store while waiting might be considered strange by other customers. It was suggested to the pharmacist that he might be underestimating the capabilities of the residents, that if residents are capable of living in a residential care facility, they certainly should be able to pick up their own medications. One resident suggested that residents who did not want to wait could call in advance so that the prescription would be ready for them when they came. The system has worked well for many months, and the residents have a positive feeling of accomplishment.

It should be emphasized that the pharmacist is a very important professional in the community, particularly in areas lower on the socioeconomic scale. Usually he is an accessible, friendly person who has the training and experience to answer many questions. Whenever possible, he should be included as part of the residential care program, for he often has useful observations to make.

Isolation is a problem not only among residents in a home, but also for the home itself. Each home often seems like a world unto itself, excluded from the rest of the community. The mental health worker who visits the home once or twice a week is often a key lifeline between the home and the outside world. A means of diminishing isolation that has been successful in one home is a periodic open house. The open house usually takes several weeks of preparation. Issues such as the date, time, theme, entertainment, food, and guests are all discussed in detail.

Perhaps surprisingly, a large number of relatives and friends always attend these evenings, and the mental health worker attempts to talk with them. So often, the typical story is that they have been through so much and are afraid of getting involved again. At the same time, they are suffering greatly from guilt. If a friend or relative shows an interest, the mental health worker attempts to help the person reduce his guilt by encouraging some contact.

The open house helps the residents get in touch with both their feelings of anger for having been rejected and their unrealistic expectations. The therapeutic work surrounding this event has tended to reopen channels to relatives and friends, often on a more realistic basis.

Another important means of dealing with the problem of isolation is encouraging residents to participate in events outside the home. Such participation means learning what facilities the community has to offer (parks, libraries, churches, concerts, points of interest, clubs, entertainment, recreation programs) and how to get there. Since residents have only limited pocket money (currently thirty-three dollars per month), transportation costs could be a major stumbling block. This problem was greatly eased in one case when the local public transit company offered a discount card (a fare of only five cents) to all disabled people, including the mentally disordered. The most important clinical issue for the residents has turned out to be a reluctance to be seen as "disabled" in public places.

A mental health worker invited an official from the public transit company to a house meeting. He discussed the reasons for offering the discount card, how to apply for the card, the various bus and railway routes, and the hours that the card was valid. The worker was somewhat disappointed at how little interest the residents seemed to have in applying for the card. At first, the lack of response was regarded as typical resident indifference. Still, it was decided to explore the issue in more detail. The residents started

asking many questions about the card: "Would it have a picture?"
"What will be written on the card?" "How large would the card
be?" Picking up on the covert issue, staff began to focus on what it
felt like to be classified as disabled and how the community looked
upon people who were so classified.

After sharing feelings about these issues, the residents did
some reality testing. "The card is not marked 'Disabled.' The community is issuing the cards not so much because the bearer is disabled, but because he has limited financial resources." Someone
pointed out that a disabled person who has adequate financing
probably would not apply. "Having a card is not necessarily a permanent status. When a person can afford full fare, he can stop
using the card."

Since the discussion, most of the residents have applied for
discount cards. Without the clinical exploration into covert feelings,
this offer by the city would probably have been used only by a small
number of residents—and it would have been concluded that the
others were not motivated.

Close Medication Management

A well-known problem in residential care facilities concerns psychotropic medications. Often the degree of psychopathology
has little correlation with the amount of medication prescribed. The
dosage seems to vary more with the physician and the home than
with the severity of illness. Homes with active programs use considerably less medication. Or, perhaps more to the point, where
less medication is prescribed, a more active program has a chance
for success. If residents are to become socially reinvolved both in
the home and in the community, they should not be maintained in
"chemical straitjackets." In homes with which mental health
workers are closely involved, the amount of medication has been
reduced by from 30 to 50 percent.

A related problem is the lack of periodic reevaluation. Medication prescribed at the time of discharge from the hospital is often
maintained for years, without reconsideration of need.

Case illustration: A forty-eight-year-old woman, who had
had three state hospitalizations between the ages of thirty-five and

forty, was discharged in 1967 to a board and care home. The diagnosis was chronic schizophrenic reaction, undifferentiated. She was placed on eight hundred milligrams of Thorazine daily. For the next eight years, she functioned well enough to remain in the home, but she required twelve to fourteen hours of sleep a day, was withdrawn, and exhibited little interest in activities outside or inside the home. Over these eight years, there had been no change in medication; the house physician had merely refilled the prescription every month. The physician was not a psychiatrist, but as the patient had no psychiatrist, he had agreed to handle all her medical problems, including psychotropic medication. He readily admitted that his knowledge of psychiatry was limited and that since these medications originally had been prescribed by a psychiatrist, he was reluctant to make any changes. He also was unfamiliar with the dangers of tardive dyskinesia and the fact that maintenance dosages of psychotropic medications can usually be given on a once-a-day basis, preferably at bedtime, to reduce daytime sedation.

As a result of this discussion, medication was changed to Stelazine and was decreased over the next few weeks to ten milligrams at bedtime. A rather remarkable change took place. The resident began sleeping only eight to nine hours a night, started taking an active interest in the home, and proceeded to spend more and more time outside of the home. She once remarked that she felt as if she had been living in a fog all those years.

We have also encountered residents who had been hallucinating and delusional but, because they did not cause disturbances, had received either no medication or a minor tranquilizer such as Valium or Librium.

Case illustration: One thirty-seven-year-old man was an agreeable resident who caused no trouble. However, he had been quite withdrawn for more than a year. The administrator assumed this withdrawal to be his normal level of functioning, although his history included employment, marriage, and a fairly active social life. The individual came to my attention because he was becoming increasingly withdrawn. He requested having meals in his room and was eating very poorly. The administrator was considering taking him back to the hospital. His psychiatrist said he would not have time to see him before his next visit in four weeks. Under my questioning, the man revealed an elaborate delusional system. Voices were warning him not to be involved with the other residents in the home and, more recently, had warned him about the food. Asked whether he had ever heard these voices before, he said that he had during hospitalization but that they had subsided. The voices returned shortly after his discharge and over the past few weeks had become increasingly intrusive. His psychiatrist (whom he sees for a few minutes every six to eight weeks) had discontinued medication about a year before because the patient was not agitated and had no problem sleeping. The question of whether his increasing withdrawal could be related to his preoccupation with his fantasy world had not been addressed.

Medication was reinstated, and within a week the man's appetite was better, he was eating with the other residents, and a possible hospitalization was averted.

The psychiatrist's role in prescribing psychotropic medication in residential care facilities must be strengthened. Presently, the psychiatrist (for homes that have one)' often works in numerous homes, seeing a large number of residents for a few minutes every month or two. To prescribe effectively, the psychiatrist must have a good understanding of the dynamics of the resident, be abreast of what is happening in the home, and have a trusting relationship with the administrator. There should be a house psychiatrist for each home, which means getting more psychiatrists involved with residential care psychiatry.

Two Approaches to Improvement

The problem of making residential care facilities therapeutic can be approached in at least two ways. The first is to attempt to improve the quality of existing facilities through individual consultation with administrators. In such an approach, mental health professionals see some administrators on a regular basis, others only as needed. The consultation sometimes centers around understanding and helping individual patients, sometimes around such issues as how administrators can establish in-house meetings, promote independence in the residents, and motivate them to participate in rehabilitation programs. The consultant recommends such specifics as providing a bulletin board for community activities and sub-scribing to daily newspapers and magazines in order to make residents more aware of the world outside the home. He also encourages the administrator to institute structured orientation procedures for new residents, to involve residents in establishing house rules (and really listen to what the residents have to say), and to stress the importance of the residents' handling their own money whenever possible. In these ways, the consultant often can be effective in lifting the air of repressiveness that so frequently exists in board and care homes.

Such consultation is important, but consultation alone does not constitute an adequate program. It is unrealistic to expect an administrator alone, aided only by consultation, to develop a therapeutic milieu and still meet all the requirements of managing a successful facility. A more realistic approach is to have mental health professionals and the administrator jointly develop and conduct the facility's therapeutic program.

The importance of professionals bringing direct treatment into the facility cannot be overemphasized. The Westside Aftercare Program in San Francisco, which was created in 1972 to provide services to long-term patients in residential care facilities, uses this approach. The residents range in age from twenty-one to sixty, the average age being forty-seven. The program originally included sixty facilities, typically with six to twelve residents, although a few homes accommodate between twenty and forty. It soon became apparent, however, that the number of facilities within the Westside Community Health Center's catchment area far outstripped the program's capacity. It was therefore decided to choose twenty homes whose administrators were most interested in working with the program and whose residents could most benefit from its services. There are approximately 250 residents at any one time who have made treatment contracts with the program and are active participants in it. As indicated in Chapter One, community care programs should not be instituted to save money. This program, with twelve full-time and seven part-time staff members, has a yearly budget of $275,000, which represents an average expenditure per resident of over $1,000.

The staff is divided into three teams. Two of the teams,

each composed of a team leader and two community counselors, specialize in working with problems of the individual residents and helping the homes incorporate therapeutic community principles into their everyday operation.

The worker assigned to a home contacts each resident at least once a month, giving the resident the opportunity to discuss privately any problems and to review progress, goals, and treatment plans. Often these sessions are used to prepare residents for more intense psychotherapy and to discuss activities outside the home that might be of interest to residents. The third team, led by an occupational therapist, handles both in-home and out-of-home activities that teach or reactivate skills needed in daily living, that is, those skills which a person needs in order to live independently. This team also teaches residents how to use and enjoy leisure time. Out-of-home activities include a weekly social evening held in a nearby church, which attracts approximately fifty residents, a rap group, a drama group, a bowling group, a writing group, and a volunteer group. The program also sponsors six field trips a week, and each home may participate in two field trips a month. An *Aftercare Newsletter* gives the homes a sense of community. Each home has a resident reporter who writes about events of the preceding month, such as visits by relatives or friends, birthday parties, arrival of new residents, departure of residents, and picnics.

Two additional staff members are assigned full time to liaison with the state hospital. They help prepare the patient for discharge to the community, find an appropriate home for him, and work with the administrator to facilitate the placement and develop a continuing-care plan. Overall, the Westside Aftercare Program is directed by a social worker. The medical director is a half-time psychiatrist who consults with the staff concerning individual homes and residents.

It should be emphasized that the residential care facilities are proprietary homes managed and usually owned by their respective administrators. A project such as the Westside Program often increases an administrator's work load by several hours a week, with no additional pay. The incentive given to these administrators is that staff members try to keep the homes operating at full capacity by filling vacancies quickly. Administrators who have full homes are much more likely to encourage independence in their residents even though independence might eventually lead to their moving out. When administrators have too many vacancies, their situation is comparable to that of the psychotherapist who tends to avoid dealing with issues leading to termination because he is concerned about not receiving new referrals.

Training Administrators. If residential care facilities are not to become community "back wards," administrators must be trained for helping their residents make a smooth transition to community life.

The administrators involved in the Westside Program in San Francisco are described as "typically black, middle-aged women who [have] converted their homes into facilities for the care of the chronically ill. The majority have had little formal training beyond high school. Although some are former nurses aides, LVNs, and the like, few have been formally trained for the demands of the job. Most see themselves in the business of helping and caring for clients, while some have the view that clients are ill to help them institute and maintain a business enterprise. Practically all of these operators have managed the care of the chronically ill for many years. They have done this by intuition, and the trial and error learning that results from varied experiences. They are aware that the general public and many social agencies have the attitude that they have a lack of concern for providing quality of care and are insensitive to their need for training. As a result, not only do they sometimes feel that the work they are doing is of little merit, but also that their residents are unworthy of receiving quality care. However, the majority continue to provide the best care available within their ability" (Rouse and Holmes, 1975, p. 11).

In July 1973, weekly meetings were begun between the Westside Program and the administrators. The sessions were not always amicable. The administrators felt that mental health professionals spent little time with the chronically ill and often were unrealistic in their expectations. The professionals tended to see the administrators as uncaring, mercenary, naïve, and generally not too intelligent. Racial antagonism existed between the administrators and the professionals, although these feelings were covert.

Despite this rather shaky beginning, it was agreed to set

up a training program that included the following points: Training would extend over a period of one year, and persons enrolled would receive six units of college credit. (See Table 1 for the course outline.) Classes would be held in the community one evening a week for three hours. Classes would be taught by a practicing professional who worked with the population with which the operators worked. A minimum of twenty operators would enroll in the class. A certificate of accomplishment would be awarded by both the San Francisco Mental Health Service and the Westside Community Mental Health Center (Rouse and Holmes, 1975, p. 12).

Those of us who took part in teaching the course soon learned that the administrators, because of their many years of experience in caring for the chronically ill, had much to teach as well as to learn. That twenty-seven of the thirty persons enrolled finished the course attests to a high level of motivation among the administrators. Further, they often had to pay others to supervise and manage their facilities in their absence. Graduation, held in the auditorium of a local Unitarian church, was an extremely moving experience. The administrators had worked hard, and they were justifiably proud of their accomplishments and full of emotion. Many were crying, and there was hardly a dry eye in the audience of over one hundred.

In residential care facilities, a new professional is emerging who was not needed in state hospitals, namely, the administrator. Among the mental health professionals today, we have the M.D., Ph.D., M.S.W., O.T., R.N., and P.T. It is hoped that the day is not too far off when the team will add R.A. (residential administrator).

Involving More Professionals. Developing programs to transform residential care facilities requires the involvement of more mental health professionals, particularly psychiatrists, who have probably been the slowest of any of the professionals to take an interest in residential care facilities. Generally, mental health professionals think that because they have not had specific training concerning residential care facilities, they have little to offer. However, theories originally designed for office or hospital practice can be applied in residential care facilities with only slight modification. For instance, theories such as those of Bateson, Jackson, and Haley

Table 1. COURSE OUTLINE

1. Mental Illness and Its History
   A. Mental Health as a Social Problem

2. Communication
   A. Verbal Communication
   B. Nonverbal Communication

3. Understanding the Human Needs
   A. The Needs of a Human Being
   B. Psychosocial Needs
   C. Human Emotion:
      1. Control of Emotion
      2. Aggression

4. Terminology

5. Human Behavior and Mental Health
   A. Normal Behavior
   B. Neurotic Behavior
   C. Psychotic Behavior
   D. Mental Health and Mental Illness

6. Deviant Pattern of Behaviors
   A. Withdrawal
   B. Aggression
   C. Projection
   D. Use of Physical Disability

7. Symptoms of Mental Disorder
   A. Perceptual Disorders
   B. Thinking Disorders
   C. Disorders of Consciousness
   D. Disorders of Orientation
   E. Disorders of Feeling
   F. Disorders of Motor Aspects of Behavior
   G. Disorders by Attention
   H. Disorders of Memory

8. Preventive Psychiatry

9. Spotting Emotional Changes

10. Crisis Intervention

11. Preventive Action

12. Self-Defense

13. Medication
    A. Tranquilizers
    B. Antidepressants

14. Alcoholism—Cause of
    A. Alcoholism as a Disease
    B. Effect on the Human Body
    C. The Heavy Drinker
    D. Detoxification

15. Community Resources for the Mentally Ill

16. Current Events in Mental Health

17. Trend in Care of the Mentally Ill

18. Nutrition
    A. Basic Four
    B. Daily Requirement
    C. Caloric Value (e.g., proteins, carbohydrates, and fats)
    D. Menu Planning
       1. Attractive Meals

19. Licensing
    A. How to Apply for License for Board and Care Home
    B. How to Keep License Up to Date
    C. What Are the Duties and Responsibilities of the Board and Care Operators?

20. Basic Record Keeping
    A. Client Records
    B. Information
       1. Gathering
       2. Distribution
       3. Confidentiality

21. Role Playing
    A. Crisis Intervention
    B. Handling Family Members
    C. Therapeutic Communication

(1956)', Lidz (1973), and Wynne and Ryckoff (1958) have a great deal of applicability here. Their theories concerning families are particularly applicable to homes with five to fifteen residents, where the social structure can be conceptualized as an "intentional" (as distinguished from natural) three-generation family and where the focus is on patterns of interaction and communication among the members.

Modern psychoanalytic theory, especially that with emphasis on ego functions (Bellak, Hurvich, and Gediman, 1973) is highly applicable to these patients, because it is these functions that are defective in the chronically ill or lost through long-term institutionalization. Ego functions such as object relations, synthetic-integrative ability, mastery-competence, autonomous functioning, judgment, and reality testing need to be learned or relearned. Training in individual dynamic psychology can be applied in working individually with residents and in helping to design optimal milieus in the homes.

Certainly hospital psychiatry, with its emphasis on group processes, therapeutic community, sociotherapy (Edelson, 1970), and the sheltered subsociety centering around the use of small problem-solving groups (Fairweather, Sanders, and others, 1969)', have extensive utility in residential care facilities. The same holds true for pharmacotherapy. If we are to minimize the number of cases in which medication is mismanaged, we need psychiatrists, and we need enough of them to give frequent and thoughtful attention to the use of psychotropic medications.

Although the training currently received by mental health professionals is generally applicable to residential care facilities, some changes would be desirable. For example, continuing the policy of a full year of inpatient hospital training for psychiatrists, with little or no residential-facility training, is questionable when there are more patients in residential care facilities today than in hospitals. Why not divide the year between hospital and residential care psychiatry? We look forward to the day when not only psychiatrists but all mental health professionals will have as a component of their training "residential psychiatry."

Closely related to the problem of attracting more psychiatrists to residential care facilities is the need for a more appropriate billing system. For example, in California, the present Medicaid system allows billing only for individual, group, or inpatient care. An additional category is necessary so that consultation services to residential care facilities, their administrators, or regular house meetings can be reimbursed.

If we can attract significant numbers of mental health professionals into residential care facilities and transform these facilities into sources of active treatment and rehabilitation, then efforts to deinstitutionalize mental health treatment will no longer mean, paradoxically, the end of treatment.

Conclusions

We are entering a new phase in the treatment of the long-term mentally ill. What differentiates this phase from so many past phases is that we do not need to develop new sets of theories, new institutions, or whole new training programs. The theories concerning individual, family, group, and milieu treatment that are used in offices and hospitals can, with surprisingly little modification, be applied in residential care facilities, where thousands of former patients are presently living. Our mental health professionals, with a slight redefinition of roles and tasks, can do their clinical work, and do it more effectively, in a residential care, rather than a hospital, setting. The major task is creating a financially viable treatment organization that is flexible, mobile, not hospital-based, and capable of working with residential care facilities to develop them into therapeutic, high-expectation, growth environments.

5

H. Richard Lamb

Gearing Day Treatment Centers to Serve Long-Term Patients

Where should the long-term patient turn for help at a time of crisis? In most cases, he can find it at a day treatment center and does not have to turn to a hospital. Should there be two kinds of day treatment centers, one for acute patients (often called a "day hospital") and another for the long-term patient? The view presented here is that there should be only one kind of facility, called a "day treatment center," which provides crisis intervention for long-term patients as well as those having their first psychotic break. This chapter is not meant to be an exhaustive exposition on the day treatment center. Rather, it will focus on those issues and techniques that bear upon the center's being an essential resource for the long-term patient.

It is all too easy to take a long-term patient and rehospitalize him when he is in crisis and becomes symptomatic. But many of these patients can be helped through a crisis situation in a day treatment center rather than in a twenty-four-hour hospital (Lamb,

1967b; Herz, Endicott, and others, 1971; Erickson and Backus, 1973; LaCommare, 1975). Since the purpose of a day treatment center should be to deal with acute, short-term problems, persons with a history of many years of mental illness are often not thought of as candidates for such an "acute" treatment center. However, if one thinks in terms of an acute episode superimposed on a chronic schizophrenic process, then the day treatment center clearly becomes suitable for many long-term patients. In such a situation, the purpose of the day treatment center is not to resolve the chronic and long-standing problem, but to get the patient over an acute crisis, or to shorten or prevent a hospitalization. In some instances, the purpose may be to mobilize and evaluate the long-term patient and prepare him for a rehabilitation program.

The day treatment center, then, will serve four types of patients: those in crisis for whom the day center will prevent a hospitalization; those in a hospital who can be discharged early only if there is an all-day community program where they can continue their treatment for a brief period prior to entering into an outpatient program; those patients who are not yet in need of hospitalization but who are at risk of admission in the near future without day center intervention; those long-term patients in the community who have regressed and need an assessment and the formulation of a rehabilitation program to bring them back into the mainstream of the community.

If the day treatment center is really serving as an alternative to hospitalization, it will contain a large number of long-term patients, each with an acute crisis superimposed. Why? Because most people with even a moderate amount of ego strength can weather the crises of life alone or with some aid from family, friends, or therapists. They do not need a full-time intensive program like a hospital or day treatment center. We are not saying, of course, that there are not many people who, under stress, develop an acute depression or psychotic episode and, after a period in a hospital or its alternative, a day treatment center, can return to their usual high level of functioning. But, generally, when a day treatment center is used for crisis intervention, we are dealing with persons with low ego strength, to a large extent the severely and chronically ill.

For that matter, the difference in both appearance and

prior functioning between acute and chronic patients at the point of admission is not as great as has often been thought (Serban and Gidynski, 1975). It has been shown that first-admitted (acute) schizophrenics and their counterpart, chronic patients, do not differ substantially on admission in terms of precipitating crisis events and mental status. Further, first-admission patients show clear-cut impairments in social and vocational functioning for a considerably longer period of time prior to their first admission than the report of sudden onset would indicate. For many, there is evidence of interpersonal and work-associated difficulties dating back to youth and adolescence (Serban and Woloshin, 1974).

The day treatment center also can serve as the hub of a network of services for long-term patients. The staff, by helping the long-term patient through the time of greatest need—acute crisis—can use the relationship and trust thus developed to involve him in a community network of ongoing rehabilitation and support. This potential will be described in more detail later.

If a day treatment center is truly to be an alternative to hospitalization, staff members must have a conviction that providing such an alternative is both possible and desirable, and they must also have strong administrative leadership and support. All must feel comfortable with having the acutely psychotic patient in the relatively unstructured (compared to an inpatient service) setting of the day treatment center. On the other hand, too much administrative pressure can be put on staff to accept all acute psychotic patients, without members feeling free to say that there are some patients who are too belligerent, too overactive, too much in need of asylum and the structure of a hospital to be manageable in a day treatment center. If it is recognized as a clinical fact that the day treatment center cannot help everyone, so that patients can be transferred to an inpatient service with a minimum of feelings of guilt and failure, then the day treatment center staff will be less hesitant to accept patients with more acute psychiatric problems. In other words, they will be secure in the knowledge that they will not have to struggle with those who prove inappropriate for this setting and in need of an inpatient service. Some may need only an occasional overnight or weekend stay on a hospital ward during crisis periods, with the day treatment center retaining primary responsibility for the patient's treatment; other patients may need an intermediate or long period of hospitalization.

Likewise, the staff should not feel that every psychotic patient has to be admitted at least initially, no matter how aggressive and out of control he may be. For many such patients, an initial brief period of inpatient treatment, followed by a referral to the day treatment center when the situation is more easily manageable, is a more practical plan (Lamb and Odenheimer, 1969). Hospital control during this initial period helps the patient go into remission sooner, and the day center staff is not taxed beyond its endurance. If pushed beyond its limits, the staff becomes increasingly resistant to treating any acutely psychotic patient. And then admission criteria become ever more selective, wittingly or unwittingly, and the population served becomes very different from that found at an inpatient service (Hogarty, Dennis, and others, 1968); the difficult-to-manage patient is no longer found in the day treatment center.

Clearly Defined Goals

What kind of treatment center are we talking about? It is important to establish a philosophy of what the day treatment center should be, so that staff members have clear objectives. The center must first and foremost be goal-oriented. Thus, the staff must at every step of the way ask themselves and the patient what goals they are striving toward. If the initial goal is to get the patient into remission, and this objective has been accomplished, then what goals are next? If the patient no longer needs the day treatment center and is ready once more to take his place in society, then he should do so. If he is unable or unwilling to strive toward further goals, then he should move on to other programs, such as outpatient psychotherapy, medication, and social clubs.

Many day treatment centers are used for simple maintenance over long periods of time (Cross, Hassall, and Gath, 1972). In many instances, a mental health program will have two kinds of day treatment centers. One will be for acute patients and the other will be for chronic patients (Beigel and Feder, 1970). In one large system the two types of day programs are described as "day hospitals," whose goal is to treat acute patients so that they can return to productive life in the community, and "day treatment centers," whose goal is to maintain and rehabilitate chronic patients (Ognyanov and Cowen, 1974). The view here is that such a dual program is a major error. The end result is that the day treatment center takes many people who probably would not be hospitalized anyway and serves basically as an enrichment of outpatient treatment. It may, for example, be serving people with personality disorders. These people usually show serious self-destructive tendencies, but they are charming, likable, intellectual, often seductive. Their early lives show much deprivation—so much so that endless amounts of staff affection cannot fill the childhood abyss. They do not change, but they do reward the staff. They make endless progress—to nowhere. Or the center may become a full-time Monday-through-Friday maintenance facility for chronic schizophrenics for periods of many years. Providing such service fosters undue dependency and regression and should not be the goal of the day treatment center, however well rationalized by patients and staff. As will be described in Chapter Seven, "Acquiring Social Competence," other programs, such as social rehabilitation clubs staffed by volunteers who receive professional consultation, can serve these people as well or better.

By admitting acutely ill patients and clarifying that the primary purpose of the center is crisis intervention and the resolution of short-term problems, the staff determines the nature of the center. For instance, it is difficult to become a babysitting service for chronic schizophrenics or a long-term facility designed to effect personality change in people with character disorders when there is a steady influx of persons in crisis whose needs must be met.

If the patient is over his acute crisis and is interested in rehabilitation, then assessment and formulation of a rehabilitation plan is a legitimate goal, as is gradually helping him to begin his rehabilitation program. But the entire rehabilitation program should not be carried on in the day treatment center. A goal of active mastery of one's environment cannot be reached in a setting that encourages prolonged passive dependency. The patient receives a mixed message that makes rehabilitation all but impossible.

The day treatment center should provide only brief periods

of care. If the patient comes to the center for more than two months, then the staff must take a really hard look at whether they still have specific goals or are simply gratifying dependency needs. Are they reinforcing the patient's sick role rather than helping him see himself as a person with strengths and self-worth? Every day is not too often to ask, "What are the goals for this patient?"

One should think of limited goals that can be accomplished in the short time available. If a patient is taken into a day hospital with the goal of resolving his core problem (that is, "curing" his schizophrenia or effecting some radical change in his character), then more is being attempted than can be accomplished in this setting in a reasonable time. Frequently, the net result of such over-ambitious therapeutic efforts is that a year, or sometimes two, elapses with very little working through as far as the core problems are concerned. Moreover, a great deal of dependency has been fostered in a setting where such long-term care is unnecessary and inappropriate. Chronic schizophrenics are particularly susceptible to this problem; many patients who are prone to institutionalism may develop excessive dependence on any other way of life outside of a hospital that does not help them to realize their potential to be independent (Brown, Bone, and others, 1966, pp. 205–207).

One does well, therefore, to think in terms of limited goals, for by limiting one's goals one can accomplish a great deal more in the long run. One may not have effected any basic change in the patient's personality structure; however, putting aside such a goal becomes irrelevant if the patient has been restored to a productive, satisfying life in the community. The more ambitious objective can then be attempted in outpatient psychotherapy (see Chapter Two).

It is important to improve and clarify one's understanding of treatment so that short-term, limited goals can be differentiated from long-term, more far-reaching goals. If staff give themselves two months or less within which to work, then, no matter how intensive the program, there is only so much that can be accomplished. Getting a patient into remission is a reasonable short-term goal; changing his basic personality is not. Assessing the patient and formulating a rehabilitation plan is a reasonable short-term goal; accomplishing the entire rehabilitation plan in the day treatment center is not. Assessing the family situation is an appropriate short-term goal. So is helping the family accept the patient's treatment and their need to be involved, or uninvolved, by resolving such issues as the family's and the patient's need to spend more time, or less time, with each other, and by helping the family members to be more aware of each other's needs or to decide to live apart. But entirely changing the psychodynamics of a family is better seen as a goal for therapy after the day treatment center.

Making the distinction between long-term and short-term goals is not difficult. So it would seem, but failure to make this distinction has been the rock upon which countless day centers have foundered, mainly because the staff has not had a clear picture of what purpose the center is to fulfill. Patients can be accepted on a trial or evaluation basis of, for example, one month. In doing this, it should be made clear to the patient that formulation of goals is important and that the period of treatment will be limited. Too often, both the patient and the family are consciously or unconsciously looking for a permanent place of asylum and haven from the pressures of the world, and perhaps from each other, and want to see any institution, including the day hospital, as such a haven. All concerned must be reminded that the day treatment center is a place for actively working out immediate problems, not a place to provide eternal care.

Psychodynamics of the Here and Now

The day treatment center, and indeed the whole network of rehabilitation services, should have a psychodynamic orientation. However, in the day treatment center, this orientation should primarily involve the dynamics of the here and now rather than those of early childhood. The pertinent questions are, for example, How much ego strength does the patient have? To what kind of pressures is he especially susceptible? What current and recent stresses have caused him to show symptoms and be in crisis now? (Detre and Jarecki, 1971, p. 132). What has gone wrong vocationally or in his relationships with the significant people in his life? Has he sustained a major loss or been under unusual pressure?

One can easily become preoccupied with the patient's psychopathology or the subtleties of the diagnosis, often at the expense of looking at the patient's pressing reality problems and helping him to deal with and adjust to the realities of life. For instance, a fifty-one-year-old, divorced osteopath had spent the last several years in a number of different hospitals. He told a very plausible and interesting tale of dealings with Cosa Nostra, described setting up a large, group, osteopathic practice, and gave a detailed narrative concerning intrigue with local and state government. This man was very convincing and articulate, and some mental health professionals involved with the case spent hours debating such questions as, Is this real or delusional? For others, the question was more one of diagnosis. Was this paranoid schizophrenia or manic depressive psychosis? At each hospital there was case conference after case conference, with the patient ultimately leaving, going to a different city, and again being hospitalized. Finally, at the third hospital, the psychiatrists involved reached a stalemate. The patient had become president of the patient government; he was running the ward and running it well. The psychiatrists, meanwhile, were still debating whether he was mentally ill and if so what his diagnosis was. The resolution of this impasse was to refer him to a day treatment center for "further evaluation." There, the staff focused directly on the realities of the patient's life. A home visit quickly revealed that the sumptuous living quarters that he described were in reality an old, unused room of an acquaintance's run-down, rambling house. A decision was made to place him on large doses of medication, and the talk of Cosa Nostra soon stopped. An evaluation by a vocational counselor indicated that the patient was not at that point able to handle the pressures of working as an osteopathic physician. It also became apparent that he did not have sufficient funds to set up a practice. It was decided that he should lower his goals, and the patient quickly accepted the idea of taking an "interim" job as a salesman. He also agreed to remain in therapy and to take medications. The reader is probably thinking that this approach is very obvious and would have been taken by anyone. However, for those caught up in this patient's psychopathology and diagnosis, it was far from obvious. And, for the patient, it meant the difference between becoming entrenched in the role of patient and taking his place in the community at a level he could handle, with the support that he needed and with a feeling he could again cope with the real world.

A Comprehensive Program

Still another temptation must be guarded against. Some day treatment centers are open only half a day, offer primarily individual and group therapy with an aggressive confrontation emphasis, and scorn the activity therapies. A very effective program for some, but most of the acutely ill schizophrenics who would otherwise go to the hospital still go to the hospital. It is important to avoid setting up the day treatment center in such a way that it excludes acutely psychotic patients.

If the center is substituting for a hospital and not just enriching outpatient treatment, then a full day is needed. Full-day service gives the patient added support, but it does not mean filling in the day with irrelevant activities. On the contrary, it means recognizing the therapeutic effects of well-planned activities, each with a well-thought-out rationale. The activities should impart to the patient skills that can be translated into his life beyond the day treatment center, in the community (Carmichael, 1964). The rationale for each activity should be understood by both staff and patients. A meaningful answer should be forthcoming when someone asks, "Why are you engaging in this particular activity?" Outings help patients learn to utilize community resources. Recreation, both indoor and outdoor, helps them learn to use their leisure time and to socialize and enjoy interpersonal relationships. Activity-planning sessions help patients learn how to organize their time in a meaningful way both in and outside the day treatment center. Role-playing sessions help them learn how to handle such situations as applying for a job, how to deal with a disagreement with a roommate, and how to conduct themselves in various kinds of social situations. A stress on translatable skills emphasizes the ultimate goal of productivity rather than dependency, activity rather than passivity, and an early return to the community.

Such meaningful activities can be extremely valuable in other ways too. Although therapeutic and educational, they are less anxiety-producing than active group therapy. The activity therapies thus permit patients to spend more time in the center without expending all their energies isolating themselves or otherwise avoiding the amount of intensive interaction and anxiety that they would encounter in a program top-heavy with group therapy.

The importance of the activity program should not obscure the fact that it is but one part, albeit a vital part, of a total program. Day treatment centers that rely only on a therapeutic milieu, an activity program, and medications are incomplete. Staff members must work with each individual patient to understand what his problems are. Once the specific problems have been identified, staff and patient together are in a position to set goals and resolve these problems. However warm, accepting, and supportive the milieu may be, it does not relieve the staff of the responsibility for taking an individualized, problem-solving approach with each patient.

Additionally it is essential to have a close working relationship with a vocational agency that has a full range of vocational services, including evaluation, testing, counseling, job placement, and a vocational workshop. This arrangement augments the center's effectiveness. It permits dealing with an important area in the patient's life, namely, the world of work, while he is still coming to the center. For those patients who will need a vocational workshop after treatment at the center, it makes possible a smooth transition from the center to the workshop. Anything pertaining to work may be frightening for the patient. But while he still has the support of the day treatment center, he can begin the vocational workshop on a part-time basis, perhaps only several afternoons a week. As he becomes less frightened and more confident, he can gradually increase his time in the workshop while decreasing his time in the day treatment center until he is full time in the workshop and has been discharged from the day treatment center. In some situations, and especially where day centers are used for long-term, simple maintenance, there is no close working relationship with a vocational agency. Rather, there is competition for patients, as if the day center needs to prove it is more therapeutic or fears it will lose all its patients to the vocational workshop and be forced to close down. A strong and enlightened administration is required in such a situation in order to maintain an overall program based on need rather than on territoriality and empire building.

Use of Psychoactive Drugs

We have talked about the day treatment center as a facility that can serve acutely ill psychiatric patients. However, the center, by its very nature, has less structure than an inpatient service. There probably will be many doors and windows, in contrast to even an open ward, where there are perhaps one or two easily monitored doors through which patients can come and go. Patients remain at an inpatient service twenty-four hours a day and do not have the daily stress of going home to what may be a difficult family situation or a situation where there is little support or contact with people. Day treatment centers usually are not set up so that enough staff can be quickly summoned to subdue, physically, a patient who has lost control. Since structure is an important ingredient in the management of the acutely ill patient, the day treatment center must compensate for these lacks in some way. One of the most important factors is a philosophy of treatment that allows the staff to use adequate doses of psychoactive drugs.

Hold off on giving medication so we can be sure of the diagnosis? By the time we are satisfied with our diagnosis, we may have a patient who needs to be hospitalized. Hold off on giving medication so that the patient's real problems can come to the fore and be dealt with? Again, we will frequently find ourselves dealing with the patient's "real problems" in the hospital. Sometimes more medication will be required in a day treatment center than at an inpatient service, in order to provide ego support and compensate for the lack of structure in the center. More medication is especially likely to be needed in the early stages of treatment.

Medication must be given when needed, which may mean when the patient is first admitted to the day treatment center or may mean responding quickly to head off or deal with a crisis. Consequently, a psychiatrist must be readily available. The psychiatrist need not work full time in the day treatment center, but he must be reachable at all times when patients are attending the center. An arrangement under which a psychiatrist comes in once or twice a day to prescribe medications or is in the center half time and unavailable the rest of the time is not acceptable if we are to deal with acutely ill patients in this setting.

Involving the Family

Probably in no other mental health setting is the involvement of the family so important. The patient goes home each night and weekend to his family. Rather than taking the easy way out and simply placing the patient in the hospital to obtain at least temporary respite from the stress of living with an acutely disturbed relative, the family is continuing to provide support and has been asked to participate in the treatment process. The family needs access to professionals who can answer their questions, acknowledge that they are under stress themselves in dealing with a difficult situation, and help them deal therapeutically with problems. Without the support and involvement of the family, treatment in the day treatment center usually will fail.

A family diagnostic interview is an important part of the evaluation of every patient in the day treatment center. Sometimes the family may be seen separately by a day staff member other than the person designated as the patient's therapist. Sometimes the patient and the family are seen together. As discussed in the chapter on individual psychotherapy (Chapter Two), the family should best not be seen by the person designated as the patient's therapist unless the patient is present.

The family diagnostic interview in which family and patient are seen together gives the staff an insight into what goes on between patient and family that can be obtained in no other way. In such an interview, interaction between the patient and his family can be observed. The patient might be totally unaware of and unable to describe some of this interaction, but observation helps the staff gauge the accuracy of the patient's perceptions of what his family is like and how he interacts with them. If staff time is available and if the family is willing, every family should be seen on an ongoing basis beyond the diagnostic interview. Further interviews bring further insights into family dynamics, and the family is able to gain additional support that may be sorely needed during difficult parts of the patient's illness. Often, even within the brief period during which the patient is in the center, both patient and family can begin to look more objectively at their relationships with each other, to make

some changes, and to think in terms of ongoing family therapy when
the patient leaves the center.

Many times the family or the patient or both are strongly
opposed to ongoing interviews. The family may believe that they are
already doing enough, or they may fear such therapy, thinking they
surely will be blamed for the patient's illness. The patient may object
because of his suspiciousness. If the family or the patient is adamantly unwilling to participate, this position should be respected.
Further attempts to involve the family can be made later on, when
they feel more ready and less threatened. In any event, the day center staff should be able to come to terms with what the family is
able or willing to tolerate and should not get into a struggle with the
family over this issue. Such a struggle may undermine the treatment or even result in the family withdrawing the patient from
the center.

Defining Roles

Nothing can be more divisive in a day treatment center than
a situation in which certain "high status" professionals have the
"high status" tasks, particularly doing individual and group therapy.
This problem need not arise if all members of the staff—nurses,
psychologists, social workers, occupational and recreational therapists, psychiatrists, and community workers—are given the opportunity to be individual therapists and to participate in and lead
group therapy. If the staff operates as a team and each case is discussed at staff meetings, there is ample opportunity for peer review
of what each staff member is doing with his particular patients. If
the professional is competent, regardless of his discipline or the
amount of his training for therapy, the therapeutic process will, in
most cases, go well, providing that everyone feels free to discuss his
cases openly at staff meetings and accepts feedback. The staff then
feels more like a team, and a minimum of energy is expended in
interdisciplinary strife and jealousy. The resultant blurring of roles
does not mean that a clear definition of roles is not needed in other
areas. For instance, the psychiatrist has expertise in medication and
certain aspects of diagnosis. Because he may have had more ex-

tensive training, he frequently will be called upon as a consultant for difficult cases. The social worker has particular expertise in dealing with families, and although many staff members may deal with families, the social worker will be called upon as a consultant in that area. The same holds true for the particular skills of the nurse, occupational therapist, and recreational therapist.

As in the case of therapy, each staff member should participate in leading the activity therapies to the extent that time and other responsibilities permit. Here, again, there is both a blurring and a definition of roles. All staff members should have some responsibility with regard to the various social rehabilitation and recreation parts of the program, but the occupational therapist and the recreational therapist should be recognized as the people with particular expertise in these areas and are the persons to whom the rest of the staff should turn for leadership and consultation.

Individual Psychotherapy

What is the role of the one-to-one relationship in the day treatment center, a facility that lends itself so easily to a team approach and the use of group therapy as a central treatment modality? Staff members may be tempted to deal with most or all issues in groups and may think that individual psychotherapy detracts from the group process. It is true that many issues are best dealt with using group processes and feedback from the patient's peers (Gootnick, 1971). However, many issues can be more meaningfully and effectively dealt with in a one-to-one situation than in a group situation. These include problems concerning sexuality or the commission of past crimes, which the patient is unlikely to discuss freely and openly if privacy and confidentiality are lacking. Another example is the situation in which a therapist is tactfully trying to help a patient lower his goals without lowering his self-esteem. In such an instance, it may be necessary to help the patient rationalize his inadequacy to handle a given work or social situation. A one-to-one situation between a skillful therapist and the patient lends itself much more easily to this process than does a group setting where, in the interests of candor and openness, the patient is encouraged by the group to face the situation "like it is." In the group,

the patient may be shattered or may react by summoning his defenses and raising his goals rather than lowering them.

There are, however, some special problems when using individual psychotherapy in a day treatment center. The relationship
may become so all-important to the patient (and therapist) that
patient and therapist become a twosome, separated from the group
milieu of the center. Further, the patient's time at the center is
limited; if one uses outpatient intensive psychotherapy as a model,
in most cases one has barely reached the opening phase of such
treatment by the time it is appropriate to discharge the patient from
the center. At this point, either one must keep the patient longer,
which is inappropriate and fosters dependency, or the patient feels
cheated and angry, because he has been seduced into opening up
painful areas that he then must leave unresolved and is now perhaps
further confused and more conflicted than before. These pitfalls can
be avoided by confining the subject matter of the individual thera-
pist-patient relationship to issues that can be resolved in the time
allowed. Such subjects include the precipitating stresses that caused
the patient to need the center, the resolution of those stresses, the
patient's feelings about giving up a life of dependency and attempting again to compete in the world, and interpersonal problems in
the day center that may typify the patient's problems with people
generally.

Another problem that frequently arises with individual
therapy is the establishment of too close a relationship between the
therapist and the patient when this relationship cannot be continued on an ongoing aftercare basis. Thus, at the time of separation from the day center, which is at best difficult and painful, the
patient finds himself further burdened by having to give up a very
meaningful and important relationship. The shift to another therapist for needed aftercare on an outpatient basis is then more difficult, and, again, the patient feels anger and resentment. Equally
important is the diversion of the patient's attention from one of
the primary goals of day center treatment, namely, resolution of the
the precipitating problems and a return to functioning in the
community.

In one-to-one psychotherapy, the therapist should try to
maintain sufficient rapport with his patient to permit accomplish-

ing the treatment objectives, but not so much that the relationship makes separation more painful than need be. He can limit the amount of time spent in individual sessions to a half hour instead of the traditional psychotherapeutic hour, thus reducing transference and lessening the intensity of the relationship. Toward the same end, these sessions can be limited to one or two per week, except in emergency situations, and should conflict as little as possible with the other activities of the center.

Relationship with the Hospital

A close working relationship with an inpatient service is necessary if the day treatment center is to provide an alternative to hospitalization. This relationship allows the day treatment center staff to attempt to manage more acutely ill patients with the knowledge that should the patient not be manageable in a day center setting, he can readily be transferred to inpatient status. For many patients, there will be times of crisis during treatment in the center when a brief period of hospitalization will be required. Knowledge that hospitalization can be accomplished with a minimum of administrative problems and without permanently giving up the case gives the staff an added feeling of confidence in dealing with acutely and severely ill persons. The patient may stay at the inpatient service for a weekend, overnight, or for several nights while attending the day treatment center during the day. If the patient needs more than just a few days of inpatient service, then he should be transferred with the understanding that the inpatient service will take over until the patient is ready to return to the day treatment center. Allowing a patient to be managed by both an inpatient service and a day treatment center for more than a few days causes a multitude of problems in communication that work to the detriment of all concerned. Further, if the patient cannot be returned to the sole management of the day treatment center within a few days, he probably needs the full-time services of the hospital. Later, when he is ready, the patient can be re-referred to the day treatment center.

In order to have a close working relationship, it is essential to have frequent and regular meetings between the inpatient and day treatment center staffs. The inpatient staff needs to understand the limitations of the day treatment center and to see that the inpatient service is meeting a critical need by providing backup, structure, and control when needed. Otherwise, the inpatient staff may feel that the facility is being used as a dumping ground and that the day treatment staff only want to handle "easy problems." It is also important to maintain constant communication about patients who are being kept for the weekend or overnight at the inpatient service so that the inpatient and day treatment staffs are working as a team and not at cross-purposes.

A misunderstanding that frequently arises is the accusation that the day treatment center staff is using the hospital as a "punishment." This charge may, of course, be correct, and if so, the problem should be pointed out to the staff. However, if a patient refuses to go along with the center's program and refuses to come on a regular basis, to participate, or to take required medication, or if he is a menace to himself or others, then the use of the hospital or even the discussion of it with the patient is actually pointing out reality— that the hospital is the only alternative to a structured day treatment center program and that the day treatment center cannot be of help unless the patient makes better use of it. Under these circumstances, hospitalization is not a punishment, but a service to the patient, his family, and society.

The close working relationship with the inpatient service also facilitates referrals of persons who have been hospitalized and are not ready to return to outpatient treatment, but whose hospitalization can be shortened by a full-time community program such as a day treatment center. The center staff must understand, however, that when a patient is referred from the inpatient service, he frequently will be experiencing painful feelings of separation from that service and may "put his worst foot forward" to appear "too sick" for the center. Thus a patient may seem relatively intact at the inpatient service and grossly psychotic and inappropriate for leaving the hospital when he appears for his intake interview at the day treatment center. If this phenomenon is understood, and if good communication is maintained between the two staffs, the patient can be helped to make the transition. Otherwise, the two staffs can become involved in a divisive disagreement about whether the patient is ready for the day treatment center, and a good working relationship may become strained.

Setting a Discharge Date

Even though the patient goes home on evenings and weekends, the day treatment center is a powerful force for gratifying dependency needs. It will often be very difficult for the patient to leave, and very frequently, the patient himself will not ask to be discharged. If the patient is allowed to stay too long, he may become institutionalized and separation may become a major problem. Therefore, it is wise to set a discharge date, based on a careful assessment, several weeks before the patient will be ready to leave the center. However, once the discharge date is set, it must be a firm and final date, not subject to change unless there is some unforeseen drastic alteration in the patient's situation, such as the death of a loved one. One of the purposes of establishing the discharge date is so that the patient no longer needs to show how sick he is in order to remain in the center. If he feels that the discharge date can be changed, then he is all the more likely to attempt to impress staff members with how sick he is. Most patients, although upset and angry at first, experience a sense of relief when the date is set. They can now begin to make meaningful plans for aftercare and for their living and work situations when they leave. It is, of course, better if the patient brings up the question of leaving and asks to leave, but if he does not, it falls upon the day treatment center staff to set the date. Frequently the patient will try to make the staff feel guilty, saying directly or indirectly, "It's cruel to send me out before I'm ready." The staff must understand that by setting the discharge date they are helping the patient go on to a higher level of functioning at a time when he is ready to do so, rather than letting him regress to a point where the process is not easily reversed.

The Center as a Nucleus

Once an acute day treatment center, with a clearly defined philosophy, has been established, it can serve as the nucleus of a community network of services for the rehabilitation and management of long-term patients. Such a network establishes a support system for long-term patients in the community and eliminates the need for state hospital "rehabilitation wards." It is logical that the day treatment center should evolve as the pivotal point for such a network, because the center is itself a community agency, unlike a hospital, and, naturally, develops close working relationships with other community agencies (Silverman and Val, 1975).

The day treatment center is well suited to serve as a nucleus for another important reason too. Patients have come to the day center in crisis, have been helped, and have come to trust and have confidence in the staff. This relationship can and should be used to involve the patients in an aftercare program run at least in part by this same staff, as opposed to referring them to professionals they do not know and with whom they may never follow through (Lamb, 1967a; Fox, 1973b). To accomplish this objective, the center could be closed to day patients one half day a week and used as an aftercare facility. Or the staff could run an evening aftercare program. Here the activity program is crucial. Such a program provides an informal, friendly atmosphere in the same place and with the same people for whom the patients still have an attachment. Consider, in contrast, the waiting room of an aftercare clinic, where one simply sits until being called into an office. As in the day treatment center, the activity program is only part of a comprehensive program that includes individual and group psychotherapy, vocational rehabilitation, medication, and work with the family.

For those patients who find it difficult to ask for help, and especially difficult when they are in crisis and most in need of it, dropping in to visit an aftercare activity program run by the day center allows them to present themselves for help while rationalizing that, "I just came back to visit." The staff comes to know the patients and their individual patterns of reacting to stress. Thus, staff members can often readily identify the early signs of exacerbation of illness while chatting informally with patients or observing their participation in activities. Crises can thus be averted, or patients can be readmitted while their problems still can be easily managed or resolved.

In addition to setting up an aftercare program in the day treatment center, the center staff should make referrals to, and maintain liaison with, vocational rehabilitation agencies, halfway houses, satellite housing programs, board and care home operators and their consultants, and social rehabilitation programs. Thus a network of services is created that can meet the ongoing vocational, housing, and social rehabilitation needs, the crises, and the continuing treatment needs of long-term patients.

It is crucial that efforts be coordinated. Coordination increases the effectiveness of each agency, and it permits the development of consensus among the various agencies about a treatment plan, so that agencies will not be working at cross-purposes. Communication about a patient's progress or lack of it in one area may enable professionals from another agency to modify their own work with the patient. Liaison contacts among various agencies must be on a regularly scheduled basis, not merely "as needed" or only at times of crisis (Lamb, 1971a). For instance, one member from the workshop staff may attend the halfway house's weekly staff meeting, a member of the halfway house may attend the aftercare staff's weekly meeting, and so on. When liaison is not regularly scheduled, communication becomes a sometime thing, to the detriment of the patient, his treatment plan, and agency interrelationships.

The web of relationships proposed here gives professionals from a group of diverse services a sense of cohesiveness. It helps cut through bureaucratic red tape and facilitates referrals and communication generally—staff members from one agency know whom to call in other agencies. Because the staff members in each agency know there is a network of supportive services to back them up, they are more confident about undertaking the treatment of difficult patients. Close coordination gives agency staffs intimate knowledge of one another's operations and problems; that knowledge, in turn, facilitates further collaboration, and staffs learn to use other agencies' services more effectively and appropriately.

But simply referring patients to these agencies is not enough. Identifying goals is important in every part of the network of services. For instance, if a patient is referred to a vocational workshop, both he and all staff members concerned should clearly understand why. Is the purpose an assessment of his ability to work? Is the workshop an opportunity to resolve problems with authority figures or coworkers on the job? The workshop staff needs to know if it is to do more than simply expose the patient to work. If it turns out that the goal is indefinite sheltered employment, then this objective should be clarified, so that large amounts of energy are not used to pursue unrealistic goals.

There is often disagreement between referring mental health professionals and the staffs of workshops, halfway houses, and other facilities as to what the goals are and how they are to be achieved. Such disagreements should be handled at regularly scheduled liaison meetings, during which both general policy issues and individual clients are discussed, so that patients are not torn by conflicts among the several agencies that are working with them.

Another principle that should be applied throughout the entire network of services is that all referrals should be taken, if appropriate, no matter how unappealing the patient might seem. An obese, middle-aged, nonverbal, uneducated patient with body odor is just as deserving of services as anyone else. In fact, one of the most frequent shortcomings in community mental health programs is that the patients treated are often those who are enjoyable to treat rather than those who may need the services most (Hogarty, 1971).

Conclusions

We have seen how a short-term, goal-oriented day treatment center can provide a true alternative to hospitalization for long-term patients. This prospect is especially likely if the center works closely with an inpatient service. Fully as important, the day treatment center also can serve as the pivotal point for a network of coordinated services including long-term aftercare, vocational and social rehabilitation, and therapeutic housing. The center capitalizes on the relationships formed with patients during acute crisis; it is difficult to duplicate a patient's trust in the agency and the staff that have helped him at a time when he was most desperate and most needy. Long-term patients need the sense of security that comes from knowing there is a support system in the community with a full range of services that can be used to greater or lesser degrees and can sustain them in what often seems to be a frightening world full of overwhelming demands. With such a system, we can not only supplant state hospitals, but also help long-term patients become, insofar as they are able, part of the mainstream of the community.

6

Cecile Mackota

Using Work Therapeutically

Despite our eagerness to make deinstitutionalization work, we have not been sufficiently prepared with plans that will help patients remain in and be treated in their communities. This chapter will examine one of these plans—the use of work as treatment. Professionals' and patients' reactions to work will be considered, as will the vocational rehabilitation counselor's role in helping patients acquire the maximum benefit from treatment.

Long-term patients run into a number of obstacles in any effort to become productive, functioning, contributing members of society. Sadly enough, the very professionals who are "helping" them frequently are the erectors of the barriers. Mental health professionals often see these patients as useless and incapable of doing productive work. Moreover, emphasis on work is considered bourgeois. To a large extent, lower-level, entry jobs or sheltered workshop activities are looked down upon and not considered worthwhile. There is much preoccupation with the "dehumanizing" aspects of the assembly line, the monotony of routine work, and the nonintellectual nature of nonprofessional work. The result is that the benefits that derive simply from working—the feeling of being productive, the sense of being needed, the social outlet in terms of one's relationships with coworkers—are all largely neglected.

If work therapy is to be used to its fullest advantage, more middle-class professionals need to guard against the tendency to view nonprofessional work in terms of their own, subjective, reaction to it. Concentrating on the aspects of work they themselves find dull, monotonous, even degrading, they often do not see that others achieve as great a sense of mastery and self-worth by success in whatever job is within their capabilities as they, as professionals, do in their own jobs. Upward-striving, high-achieving professionals must recognize that their patients' values may be different from theirs and that their patients do not necessarily consider tasks requiring less cognitive skills demeaning. Doing any job well is generally highly regarded in circles other than those of mental health professionals.

A situation comes to mind of a young man recently discharged from a state hospital who was able to leave our workshop after only three months and get a job as a dishwasher in a large, busy cafeteria. Understandably proud, he came to report this to his aftercare group. The response of the group leader was, "Isn't that great! That will help you to get a better job later." Insensitive to the satisfaction his client was feeling, the professional in one sentence destroyed his joy by downgrading his achievement.

Some Conceptions and Misconceptions

It was observed in Chapter Five, on the day treatment center, that this facility should not be used as an ongoing, lifelong resource for long-term patients. The alternative, which is much more appropriate and does not foster regression and undue dependency, is one which combines work therapy and social therapy in a mix that is tailored to the needs of each patient. But before we can use work therapeutically, we must wade through a number of misconceptions.

There is not, as many have supposed, a clear relationship between work capacity and degree of emotional recovery; that is, the ability to obtain a job and perform it does not require a certain degree of wellness. Some of the sickest and most disturbed people are able to work, some marginally, some with a high degree of competence (Olshansky, 1968). Also, it is often assumed that people have to be socialized before they are able to go to work, that they have to achieve a high enough level of social skills to get along with other people on some basis of reciprocity. As Olshansky has pointed out, this is not necessarily the case. Some ex-patients can act appropriately within a structured work situation when cues are available to guide them, but may be immobilized and confused by the lack of structure in a social situation. Others may achieve a high level of social skills but be unable or unwilling to work.

Work is seen by many clients as an activity in which they are not required to exercise social skills. This makes it more comfortable than other activities. For instance, one client said, "On my job I don't have to be me." What she meant was that while she was working, the nature of her job defined her; she was a "cashier," and all her social anxieties could be put aside while she concentrated on the tasks of a cashier. She understood clearly what she had to do and felt competent to carry out the specific activities connected with the job. By contrast, she was lost in a social situation where she saw herself as having to chart her own course and meet standards that seemed to her frighteningly amorphous.

A related and important point is that sometimes, for the severely and chronically ill, stressing socialization is contraindicated. For example, a withdrawn young man had always had difficulty relating to others in social situations. He could, however, work effectively as an electronic assembler, because his interaction with other workers was minimal and could be limited to job matters. In the course of therapy, the patient was encouraged to develop social skills and to try them out on the job. Within a short period, he had quit his job and required hospitalization. After some time, he was able to express the deep fears socialization had aroused in him, because he could not determine what degree of socializing was appropriate to the various situations in which he found himself. He felt that he had completely lost control and became so upset that he had to flee from the situation. The expectation that long-term patients will learn to socialize is not always realistic, and many have demonstrated that they can function much more adequately when not called upon to develop and use social skills.

Frequently, having gained a degree of self-confidence from being successful on a job, clients can very gradually begin to devote their energies to performing better in social situations. For this reason, some clients should be considered for very early placement in a work situation rather than in a day center or any other treatment requiring free social interaction with others. Such placement allows them to work on their interpersonal interactions gradually, while engaged in a structured work task.

Olshansky (1972) refers to the myth of "transitionalism," the myth that almost every disabled person can be or wants to be rehabilitated. There are many disabled persons who, for a variety of reasons, cannot be rehabilitated into regular competitive employment. They lack either the capacity or the will to meet the rigorous demands of most employers. For this group, permanent sheltered workshops are needed. It is often the professionals rather than the clients who believe that permanent sheltered work is not good. Having a reason to get up in the morning, a place to go where one can be useful and productive and earn money and where one has friends and feels accepted, can be a tremendously important factor in the life of a person for whom the alternative is sitting in his residential care home watching television.

We cannot, however, automatically assume that all long-term clients will remain in need of a sheltered workshop. Some clients for whom we would predict little improvement will surprise us and ultimately go on to competitive employment. There should be no limit on how long clients can remain in the workshop and no pressure on them to leave. When they are ready to move on, they find ways to let us know.

Professionals need to understand that work therapy must have a well-thought-out rationale. Using work only to provide a daytime activity accomplishes little in the way of therapy. How serious and important the professional feels the work task is and how he communicates his attitude, consciously or unconsciously, to the client, has a profound impact on how effective the work therapy is. To begin with, the professional must maintain the same attitude whether or not the work involves competitive employment. If the task the client is doing is made to seem of little consequence, he cannot see it or himself as being valuable. The mental health professional can get across in verbal or nonverbal ways his reaction to low-level, low-pay jobs, and he needs to guard against such disclosures in reacting to his patients' work activities. For most of his patients, work has been an important, integral part of their lives, and in our culture, our work still remains one of the major means by which we take our place in the mainstream of life.

Whether we are talking about a sheltered workshop or some other work setting, it should be emphasized that in work therapy it is important to understand psychodynamics and that we are using sophisticated techniques even though at first glance they may appear simple. Work therapy is often seen as nonintellectual by mental health professionals, and, because it does not involve an intellectual discussion of psychodynamics, a superficial look at this type of therapy may confirm that opinion. However, a number of important concepts underlie work therapy.

Mastery is one of these concepts. The client's feeling of accomplishment and his knowledge that he has been able to perform in a task whose value is proven to him (because he has been paid money for it and because his work has resulted in a useful product) give him a sense of mastery, a feeling that he is not powerless and helpless in the world. He can begin to discard the dependent patient role and take on the identity of a worker. Contrary to what is thought in many circles, the client must receive vocational counseling throughout this process, in order to give substance to what he is doing and so that his gains or losses may be evaluated and consolidated. The counselor's role will be discussed in greater detail later in this chapter.

Also involved is the concept of high expectations. This concept does not require that every client achieve competitive employment. Rather, for each client, the expectation is that he perform at the highest level of which he is capable. For example, in a workshop, if the highest possible level for a particular client is 50 percent of what workers in industry would be able to achieve, then 50 percent is a high expectation for this particular client. But if he is able to achieve 50 percent, we should not be satisfied, or let the client be satisfied, with 25 percent. Clients respond to these expectations in a positive way in terms of both their achievement and their self-esteem, and the professionals working with them need to communicate clearly what the expectations are. An attitude of high expectation tells the client in a meaningful way that others see him as more competent then he himself supposed and that he is capable of achieving at a higher level.

The same principle of high expectations should be applied to the client's behavior in any type of training or work activity. If we give him the clear, consistent message that we expect a certain kind of performance from him and will not accept craziness or apathy or a rationalization such as, "I can't do that, I'm handicapped," then we are likely to get a better level of performance and a healthier response. It is important that this attitude be enunciated as well as implied by our actions.

Work therapy is directed to the healthy part of the person. The aim is to maximize his strengths and not to focus on his psychopathology. Work therapy focuses on reality factors rather than on intrapsychic phenomena and on changing behavior rather than on changing basic character structure. Work therapy may seem mundane to many in the field, but it can make the difference between a life of regression, dependency, and depression, on the one hand, and a life with considerable gratification and a sense of mastery, on the other.

An example will illustrate some of these points. A workshop client is sitting at his work station hallucinating and not working. The foreman says to the client, "Stop talking back to the voices and get back to work." The foreman is talking to the well part of the ego. He is applying the concept of high expectations by conveying to the client that he is capable of being productive and is expected to strive to realize his potential. He is emphasizing to the client his identity as a worker rather than as a patient. He is using a direct approach that reaches the client. He is helping the client achieve control. Further, he is indicating to the client that he cares about him, instead of simply allowing him to sit there preoccupied with his psychotic symptomatology.

The Workshop

One of the most effective settings for work therapy is the sheltered workshop. Insofar as is possible, the workshop should be like any other work situation in industry. Thus, it should be a freestanding, factorylike facility in an industrial area, and it should have real work that is subcontracted to it by real customers from business and industry. Here clients are seen and, more importantly, see themselves, as workers, not patients. A workshop in a hospital or clinic setting simply becomes a work-oriented day treatment center. A patient's behavior conforms to his surroundings. A patient seen in a day center in the morning may display sick behavior. In the afternoon, in a workshop where normal worker behavior is expected, that same patient may be indistinguishable from factory workers everywhere.

Psychiatric treatment, as such, should not be available in the workshop location. Clients need to get the clear message that the work setting is not a place where illness is dealt with or where there is any reinforcement of the role of patient. Rather, here the rewards are directed exclusively to the well behaviors displayed. The effectiveness of work therapy diminishes if the distinction between work and treatment facilities is blurred.

A number of other lessons have been learned by experience with chronic patients. Frequently, a workshop program for long-term clients is set up in a segregated, "terminal workshop" or "work activity center," thereby establishing a self-fulfilling prophecy. Since the person in the terminal workshop is expected to be there indefinitely and is labeled as a "low producer," he proves these two expectations to be correct. On the other hand, if long-term clients are integrated with more transitional and less chronic clients, many of them are able to increase their productivity to unexpectedly high levels. As has been observed in many settings, the more poorly functioning members of the group tend to bring themselves up to the level of the better functioning members (Fairweather, 1964). The more transitional and better functioning clients serve as models and have a positive effect on the long-term clients.

Transitional workshops are reluctant to admit that clients remain in their workshops for long periods. The fact is that every workshop has some clients who do not move and, indeed, provide stability for a workshop. They cannot function outside the workshop because they need the protected setting and the support it provides. In the workshop, however, their work may be up to the standards of industry. Further, they are essential to the workshop, for they are reliable, they will do any job, they teach new clients coming into the shop, they take responsibility, and they frequently are used as lead persons. They serve an important function in the workshop in terms of their productivity, their leadership, and the role models they provide—and they know it. They are functioning at their maximum capacity, and they stay out of hospitals. The workshop thus enriches their lives and enables them to make a good adjustment in the community.

Another very important lesson is that there is a direct relationship between the value of the workshop experience and how well the purpose of the assignment is clarified. The patient who does not know specifically what he is doing in the workshop will gain little. A chronically ill person cannot assimilate such a global purpose as "to improve work habits." He can, however, understand and make sense out of such reasons as: "To test out how many hours you can work at one stretch." "To help you learn to take orders from your boss, so you can keep your next job." "To help you control your symptoms." "To see if you really want to work." Not only does the patient have some structure to depend on and a defined purpose, but the workshop staff, too, can be much more effective with such clarity. Everyone knows what to do, knows what to work on with the client, and has a basis for evaluating his progress. If he is there to improve his ability to follow orders, for instance, the number of times the client succeeds can be measured and the point when the problem has been eliminated can be determined. If inability to tolerate staying at a work station is given as the reason for the referral and the client's behavior reflects no such problem, then other reasons can be sought for the patient's job failures. The staff can deal with facts instead of relying on supposition.

It hardly need be said that the more the patient shares in determining the goals of the placement, the more he will benefit. He will see himself as having some mastery over plans for his life. He will know what to expect instead of being confronted with a fear of the unknown. Many patients who are sent to the workshop, but who delay appearing and soon leave again, probably do so because they are vague about why they are going and believe they are following a plan imposed on them by others. Under these circumstances, they enter the shop with a feeling of powerlessness and with little hope for themselves. Every effort should be made to arrange for the patient to visit the workshop at least once before firm plans are made, and, if possible, he should meet the foreman with whom he will be working. He should then share in the determination of whether the workshop will help to meet his needs. Of course, in some instances, the long-term patient needs direction. Sometimes the patient is too depressed or confused to make such a decision and needs to be temporarily "lent" some ego strength and instructed to attend the workshop. When used with discrimination, this directive method is often the most helpful for regressed patients.

In formulating goals, the question of whether it is likely that the patient can reach them must be given careful consideration. Very often it is necessary to set small, interim goals, without naming or even setting the ultimate goal. Thus a first goal might be as simple as remaining in the workshop for two hours without asking to go home. When this goal is accomplished, another, slightly more sophisticated plan can be made, and so on, until the maximum potential is reached. By this method, the patient can experience a number of successes, each one contributing to an enhancement of his self-esteem. When, on the contrary, the goals are impossible for him to reach, he is likely to react with withdrawal and depression. It should be emphasized that this kind of open-ended flexibility does not limit the final result in any way. A patient is free ultimately to go on to competitive employment, or not, depending on his own capacity.

Throughout the workshop experience, long-term patients need continuing assessment, reassessment, support, and, where appropriate, help in making vocational choices and planning for employment. This is the function of the vocational rehabilitation counselor, who works with the workshop staff as well as with the patient to ensure that the service his client receives is meaningful and suits his needs.

Vocational Rehabilitation Counseling

The attitude that vocational rehabilitation counselors should play a relatively unimportant part, or no part, in the treatment of the long-term patient is fairly common. The basis for this point of view is the fact that a substantial percentage of these patients will not enter the competitive labor market. However, the intrinsic value of work therapy makes quality rehabilitation counseling a necessity whether or not the goal is regular employment. Certainly, how much counseling, what kind, and when it is utilized will depend on the needs of the individual patient. This would be true in working with any category of patients. But work therapy attempted without the particular skills of a rehabilitation counselor has greatly diminished potential.

In what ways can the counselor work more effectively in this area than other helping professionals? It is true that what the counselor does often seems indistinguishable from what psychotherapists do. The important difference, however, lies in the counselor's orientation to the occupational aspects of life, his special knowledge in the field, and his focus on accomplishing behavior change with regard to work. Purposely setting aside other areas of the person's life, the counselor focuses on vocational planning and vocational activities. His conviction is, however, that successes in these areas enhance other therapy and facilitate change in other facets of the client's life.

The Committee on Psychiatry and Social Work of the Group for the Advancement of Psychiatry (1973)˙ lists among the crucial ingredients of mental health a feeling of self-esteem, a sense of inner resources and competence, and a capacity and liking for independent functioning. One would be safe in assuming that every long-term patient could be judged as lacking in these qualities. The vocational rehabilitation counselor, as well as other mental health professionals, directs his energies toward helping the patient meet these criteria, but the counselor uses work as the therapeutic tool.

A frequent question is, What kind of patient should be referred for vocational rehabilitation services? Counselors are apt to reply that anyone who expresses any interest at all and who can get to a facility should at least have the opportunity to be considered for these services. Assessment by a professional vocational rehabilitation counselor may bring different results than the referring therapist might have expected. Sometimes, the patient who appeared to the therapist to be a questionable referral seems highly appropriate in the judgment of the counselor, and vice versa. Counselor and therapist see the patient from different perspectives. Moreover, the patient may present himself very differently to the counselor. When the patient sees a therapist in a psychiatric setting, he usually will conform to the role expectations of his environment and behave like a patient, so his employment potential may not be evident. On the other hand, he may be expressing a desire to work to the therapist because he wants the therapist to perceive him as a person who wants to work, although in actuality he may be extremely fearful of work and not ready to consider it. In his discussion about work with the vocational counselor, the patient himself may see these realities, or they become plain to the counselor.

Although referral of the chronic patient should be made as early as possible, it should not be made at an unpropitious time. The patient can derive little benefit from vocational rehabilitation if his energies are totally involved with a divorce, a separation, the loss of a loved one, or a major change in his life-style. The therapist, however, should be sensitive to the very beginnings of recovery from crisis and help the patient to become involved in work activity before he settles into a life pattern of apathy and inactivity.

The vocational rehabilitation counselor will be involved with the long-term patient throughout the entire rehabilitation process. In his early contacts with the chronic patient, he probably will need to take a more active, authoritative role than he would normally assume with other clients. It may be some time before the severely disabled client can be expected to take positive action on his own— and an even longer time before he allows himself to believe that there is any hope that he can operate effectively. A more client-centered approach should, of course, be taken as soon as the patient is able to take on self-direction.

Following referral, counselor and patient will be assessing each other and working together to determine immediate plans. Most often for the long-term patient, the workshop is a good beginning. At this point, the counselor's concern will be that the patient be clear about what he hopes to accomplish in the workshop. The counselor will have reviewed the patient's employment history and made some judgments about employment potential as well as which behaviors would have to be adjusted before successful and satisfying employment could be reached. With these judgments in mind, the counselor can help the patient identify problems to be dealt with in the workshop. To repeat, the counselor must be cautious in this determination and plan for simple goals that the patient will have no trouble in reaching.

During the time the patient is in the workshop, regular meetings with the counselor will be scheduled so that progress or lack of it can be assessed and new goals can be set. It will be advantageous for the counselor to be very open with the client, because the client is then likely to respond with a similar openness and to deal with real issues. To illustrate, a workshop client on medication producing tremulousness if taken alone consistently came to the workshop without taking his side-effect medication. He would say he had forgotten and would have to go home to take it, thus losing several hours of work time. The counselor felt free to say, "Several times in the past two weeks you have missed hours of work because you had to return home for your medication. I think you are trying to tell us you don't want to be here." With the situation clearly spelled out and in the open, the patient could then talk about his real concerns—not really wanting to work, feeling resentment because he felt his wife and therapist were forcing him to come, and the fear that eventually he would have to face a job that was beyond his capabilities.

Schizophrenics sometimes can tolerate closeness in only very small amounts, and contacts may be very short and limited to the workshop floor. For instance, one "success story" client, who has now been employed for four years, was at first unable to tolerate as short a period as ten minutes in the counselor's office. She would sit on the very edge of the chair and protest continually that she wasn't worth the counselor's taking any time with her. Because of her evident discomfort, the client was seen only during work, for a short conversation or greeting. It was not until she came to the counselor's office and requested an appointment that regular interviews were set up. Even then, they were never more than fifteen to twenty minutes long. Eventually she was able to stay in the counselor's office without discomfort.

Another unorthodox technique was used with this same client. She was so convinced of her worthlessness that she was extremely reluctant to go out on job interviews. "No one would have any use for me or want me." When, in the counselor's opinion, she was ready for job interviews, arrangements were made for the prospective employer to see her at the workshop. The client agreed, on condition that it be made perfectly clear that she was a slow producer, "so that they don't hire me on false pretenses." The counselor pointed out to the employer, however, that the client was a dependable worker, quick in learning new tasks. Only under these circumstances could she tolerate being interviewed. The employer saw samples of her work, was impressed by her record and evaluations in the shop, and hired her. She is still there four years later and still telling her therapist that she is going to be fired any time for being so slow. When last contacted, the employer was very pleased with her work.

This example serves to further demonstrate that with the long-term patient, classic techniques are not always appropriate and that the counselor as well as other professionals needs to consider and try other methods that may produce better results.

A rather common outcome of the client-counselor relationship in work with long-term patients is the discovery that a patient who has the intellectual capacity or aptitude for certain careers has neither the emotional strength nor the personality characteristics to succeed in those fields. An in-depth knowledge of occupational requirements is necessary to reach and act on this conclusion. Counselors are aware of the ingredients that go to make up the work environment of the various occupations and the essential personality traits required. Conversely, knowledge of the client will suggest to the counselor which occupational fields will be compatible with his personality.

Sometimes this knowledge is used to reinforce the appropriateness of the client's current job, and psychiatric therapy can then focus on the real problems without resorting to "geographic therapy" (change of jobs). An excellent example of such reinforcement is a forty-two-year-old engineer, a schizophrenic who had been in therapy since the age of fifteen. He had been able to achieve a very good employment history in spite of the degree of his illness. He was employed on an experimental electronics project, working largely alone in a situation that was low-key and relatively unpressured. He was referred for vocational counseling and testing to find another kind of work he could do because he believed a recent exacerbation of his illness was caused by his job. Following counseling and a battery of vocational interest and aptitude tests, it was clear that the job in which he was engaged was uniquely suited to him. He and his therapist then were able to explore other areas and pinpoint why he was particularly troubled at that time.

With many long-term clients who express a desire to work, it will become clear that there is only a very remote possibility or no possibility that work outside a sheltered setting can be considered. Here, the counselor's role will be to alleviate anxiety about "not progressing" and give support to the patient in what he is doing in the workshop. In this instance, the counselor's attention to the details of a continuing evaluation reassures the client of the value of his work activity. Furthermore, in this way, the door is left open for future spontaneous change and improvement that occurs even in very regressed clients.

It is noteworthy that some clients have articulated the belief that going to work is their only way out of "the mental health system." Working is so equated with normalcy in our society that it becomes a major criterion of "wellness." For this reason, therapists who make use of vocational rehabilitation services add another important dimension to their treatment of chronic cases.

Use of Vocational Rehabilitation Services

It is the wise therapist who is aware that he cannot be expected to be knowledgeable in everything and can comfortably refer his patients to specialists in areas outside of his own training. The vocational counselor is outside of his role in attempting psychotherapy leading to personality reconstruction, and he does a disservice to his client if he attempts it. So it is with the therapist who attempts vocational counseling and career selection; he is not serving his patient as well as he might by a judicious referral to a person with vocational rehabilitation skills.

In referring a patient for vocational rehabilitation services, some therapists specify a particular activity: "Needs sheltered workshop," for example, or, "Place in training to be a landscape gardener's assistant." However, better results can be obtained if the therapist simply refers for a vocational evaluation and whatever services then appear indicated. In this way, he allows the counselor and the patient to work out vocational plans unhindered. The patient who arrives unannounced at the vocational services center, lunch in hand, prepared to enter the workshop "because the doctor sent me" is rarely able to consider other plans without a great deal of difficulty. As already mentioned, from the perspective of a vocational rehabilitation counselor, the patient may look almost totally different than he appeared to the therapist, and the workshop may not be the best plan for him.

Somewhat along the same line is the encouragement by the therapist of a particular vocational aspiration for the sake of supporting any positive activity on the part of his patient. Frequently, and understandably, the therapist sees an interest in a vocation as a healthy sign, takes that interest at face value, and fosters it without any real discrimination. For instance, the patient may say he wants to be an electronics technician, and the therapist agrees that the idea is a good one. This endorsement from the therapist without any determination of the patient's fine finger dexterity, mathematical ability, patience with minute detail, or even whether or not he is colorblind, usually results in the patient's adamantly pursuing that career selection no matter how inappropriate. Rather, the therapist could have responded, "I'm glad to see that you are thinking along the lines of considering employment. Why don't you discuss this with your vocational counselor. She might also have some other ideas you would want to consider." In this way, the door would have been left open for other options.

It is easy to take a simplistic approach to the choosing of a career and the preparation for it. Questions constantly heard by counselors—"Why can't he be a machinist?" or "Why can't he be a lab technician?" or "Why can't he be an electrician?"—indicate just how little the average person really looks at what is involved. Not only must there be the more obvious match between the occupation and ability, aptitude, and interest, but the patient must go through the whole painful process of facing up to weaknesses and limitations. The difficulty experienced by most long-term patients in making decisions must be overcome, and then a commitment to a course of action must be made. Most often, altering maladaptive behavior and attitudes must be the first step. With the chronic patient, this whole process is very slow, and if it is hurried, it is not likely to succeed. Thus, in using vocational rehabilitation services, the referring therapist should caution himself as well as the patient that careers are not pulled out of a hat and patience must be exercised by all concerned.

This caution is particularly necessary when patient and therapist have unrealistic ideas of the capabilities and readiness of the patient. A good example of this is a referral of a forty-seven-year-old housewife with the notation "Needs a job right away to get her out of the house." This woman had a twenty-year history of abuse of barbituates and other tranquilizers and sleeping pills and had not worked since she was twenty-one. She had no work skills, appeared withdrawn and fearful, and had no idea of the kind of work she would like to do. She came prepared to have the counselor produce some magic results, and when these were not forthcoming she gave up and did not keep further appointments.

Further, by making this type of referral and implying that the counselor has not responded well if an immediate job is not found, the therapist places the onus for the patient's lack of success on the vocational counselor. Counselors who have been in the field long enough can bounce the guilt back and comfortably refuse to take it on, but for many counselors, this can be a devastating experience. Certainly it makes good teamwork with that therapist impossible.

Teamwork is a significant consideration in the use of vocational rehabilitation services. Those therapists who have trouble "sharing" their patients with other professionals deprive these patients of the full benefit of all the services available to them. Counselor and therapist can significantly enhance each other's work if they are willing to collaborate fully in planning for and treating long-term patients. Even then, unless there is real communication, counselor and therapist may be working with the client on goals that are at odds with each other. Neither goal can be reached under these circumstances.

Teamwork makes it possible for the therapist and the counselor to get the kind of feedback from each other that takes their work out of the realm of speculation. Through communication with the therapist, the vocational counselor knows when additional pressure in the patient's vocational program would be inadvisable because of events in his life that render him unable to tolerate added pressure or new activities. The therapist, in turn, knows how the patient is really responding in a work situation. Each must commit himself to keeping the other aware of new information, changes in the patient's life situation, and changing goals in order for their work to be really effective.

An ever recurring complaint of counselors is that therapists refer only the poorest functioning patients, whom "they don't know what else to do with." Sometimes this complaint reflects a reluctance to work with these patients. However, there are many long-term patients who are bright, animated, and capable of benefiting from vocational rehabilitation services but do not get referred. Often they are working and having problems on the job. Vocational counselors, with their intimate knowledge of the work environment, may be able to offer services that will keep the patient on the job or help him function better on the job. If indicated, the counselor can make a realistic assessment of the patient's options regarding other kinds of work.

For the better functioning patient who has not made a career selection or whose selection may be questionable, a referral to a vocational rehabilitation service may prevent needless hardship. The counselor's input based on his knowledge about occupational fields can be invaluable. He can assess the client's suitability for certain occupations in terms of both his temperament and his aptitudes and skills. Thus the patient is helped to avoid setting himself up for the failure that is bound to result from pursuing an impossible goal. It is far more fruitful for the referral to be made during the career selection process rather than after failure has occurred. All of the chronic patient's fears about himself have then been confirmed, and it may be a long time before the damage can be reversed.

In a previous article (Lamb and Mackota, 1975, p. 23), a case example was cited that clearly illustrates this point.

> Many clients have the intellectual ability or the aptitude
> to do a number of jobs which might be devastating to them

emotionally. They can do very well through a lengthy and expensive training program only to fail miserably when they are on the job. An example comes to mind of a young woman with artistic ability, fine coordination and with an expressed interest in working with people. Her choice of an occupation was cosmetology. She was bright and creative and completed the course easily, earning the praise of her instructors for her work. But in the rather intimate, letting-hair-down atmosphere of a beauty shop she was lost. She found it extremely difficult to share with the other operators in the glib, "anything is discussed" way they have, and her need for privacy made her suspect. She could not become part of the group and she had the same difficulty with the careless, quick, surface intimacy the customers expected. Had she been counseled early she would never have gone into this field. She did not possess the temperament and personality characteristics demanded in this job, and she would not have been exposed to an outcome so predictable to a skilled counselor.

After several disastrous experiences in beauty shops, the young woman was referred to our agency by her therapist. She said she was seeking help in finding a new occupation. She was very bitter about her past employers and depressed because her own cataloging of her skills still pointed to cosmetology. Following a number of counseling sessions, it was possible for the client to face the reality that working in a beauty shop was not for her. With much support she could drop her defensiveness and recognize elements in her personality which contributed to her lack of success. More important, she could explore other areas where she could use her skills and also meet the full expectations of the job.

Vocational testing and consideration in counseling sessions of a wide range of occupations still revealed a definite aptitude and preference for work with and creatively styling hair. This led to job applications at wig manufacturing plants and a job as a wig stylist at one of them. Much of the time she works alone and the job never requires working with customers. The placement has been a successful one in terms of job satisfaction and stability.

Counselors thus need to be fully aware of the ingredients that go into making up the work environment of the various occupations. It is of greatest importance that these ingredients be considered in judging the suitability of an occupation. Just as it was seen that the girl mentioned above could deal with the technical aspects of the job but not its social environment so each occupational setting must be understood in terms of its own unique environment.

The authors believe that no one enters a field of work "accidentally" and that the main element in a person's remaining in a given career is his own personality. There really are types of people in the sense of having particular personality traits in common, who become waitresses or school teachers or counselors. Although persons in these fields can be very different there are basic traits they share or they would be in some other work. The counselor's skill is exhibited when he helps his clients see themselves realistically and choose the fields that suit their own personalities.

Conclusions

Work therapy with long-term patients is an extremely effective activity that not only helps these patients remain in the community, but makes their lives more meaningful. It contributes to their mental health by increasing their feelings of self-esteem and mastery over their lives, and it often leads to their achieving independence through employment. It is viewed by many patients as the only means of extricating themselves from the mental health system and shedding their identity as mental patients. It is equally effective for those who will go into competitive employment and those who will remain in sheltered work situations.

Mental health professionals need to extend their use of vocational rehabilitation services in order to make available to their patients all the options open to them to improve the quality of their lives. In so doing, referring therapists need to be aware that they can have a profound impact on the effectiveness of work therapy by the ways in which they use these services and by their attitudes and the importance, or lack of it, that they attach to the work activities of their patients.

7

H. Richard Lamb

Acquiring Social Competence

A central theme of this book is that wherever and whenever possible, people should be helped to cast off the patient role and see themselves as citizens like any others in the community. Insofar as possible, we should normalize the environment in which they work and play. Thus, we should try to set up programs outside of mental health settings. Long-term patients can become as dependent on a community mental health center as they were on the hospital.

The whole area of acquiring social competence (usually called "social rehabilitation") lends itself readily to this approach. As will be shown throughout this chapter, the helping persons with whom the patient has direct contact should be teachers, volunteers, recreation department personnel, and college students. The long-term patient needs maximum contact with regular members of the community. In the social rehabilitation process, as distinguished from other aspects of treatment and rehabilitation, mental health professionals can best serve as consultants.

Social Rehabilitation in a School Setting

When the many thousands of long-term psychiatric patients began streaming out of the state hospitals into the community, it

115

quickly became clear that they were woefully deficient in the basic skills of everyday living. More recent experience in community mental health programs, with young chronic schizophrenics, has revealed similar problems even though these patients have not spent long years in state hospitals. Their deficits in ego functioning include not being able to achieve mastery over their environment. Much of their difficulty in adjusting to the community has to do with not knowing such things as the essentials of managing their money and budgeting; how to use banking services; how to utilize the resources available to them in the community; how to use their leisure time; the fundamentals of nutrition, meal planning and shopping; how to use public transportation; the essentials of grooming, personal hygiene and sex education; and the very basic social amenities that make the difference between a life of isolation and having friends. For many patients, knowledge and skills in these areas not only make a great difference in the quality of their lives but make the difference between being able to live independently in the community and living in a hospital or at a very low level of existence in a residential care home.

It has been found by some that the most effective way to impart these skills systematically to long-term schizophrenic patients is to use an educational model, that is, to set up classes and to have a curriculum (Glasscote, Cumming, and others, 1971; Ludwig, 1971; Spiegler and Agigian, in press). Unfortunately, these programs have been set up in mental health settings such as hospitals, day treatment centers, and aftercare programs. But keeping long-term patients in mental health settings promotes dependency on these settings rather than independence. These considerations led the author to set up a social rehabilitation program to teach the basic skills of everyday living not only on an educational model, but in an educational setting.

The local high school district was approached and readily agreed to sponsor the course as a regular part of their adult education program and pay for the teacher. We looked for a credentialed teacher who would be flexible enough to teach a group of students who present somewhat different problems than those normally encountered in classroom situations. The teacher who was hired had had most of his experience in teaching classes of emotionally handicapped children and was thus prepared to deal with crises in his classroom and with students whose emotional problems interfere with learning. The course is entitled "Personal Growth Education." We would have preferred to use a regular school classroom, but daytime classroom space was not available for the eight hours a week needed for this course. However, the local chapter of the American Red Cross made one of their classrooms available to us for the first year. In the second year, the course was moved to a community recreation center. At both locations there was no charge for the classroom. And at both the atmosphere is very definitely noninstitutional. Before each course, the teacher speaks to aftercare personnel and social clubs for long-term patients. Many of the students have had the course recommended to them by their therapists. Also, the course is offered in the regular adult-school catalog. But however the potential students have heard about the course, they enroll for it as they would for any other adult-school course.

Encouraging Student Involvement. A key element in this course is encouraging student involvement. The first class of each course in Personal Growth Education is devoted to having the ten to twelve students make up a "needs list." The students are asked what they see as their needs in terms of the knowledge and skills of everyday living. All of the needs volunteered by the students are put up on the blackboard, and in the ensuing discussion the class decides which of the topics are most important for the group as a whole. Priorities are assigned by the class, and the topics receiving priority are given the greatest emphasis during the course. It is further understood that the needs list can be revised as the course goes along, and the list is posted where it can be seen at each class. Thus the teacher and students together draw up the curriculum. The importance of the students' participation cannot be overestimated, for in addition to learning the specifics of the course, they also learn to take responsibility. For those persons who have spent long periods in state hospitals, responsibility is a new experience, since they have lived in an environment where most decisions were made for them. For such students, and also for the students who have not yet become "institutionalized" in state hospitals, the knowledge that they have responsibility for what happens in the classroom setting is translatable to other areas of their lives. Many long-term patients feel that they cannot exercise any control over what befalls them and have, therefore, no responsibility for their fate; they see themselves as victims. Learning that they can take responsibility for what happens in a class thus becomes especially meaningful, for it helps them see that they have control over what happens to them elsewhere too. What occurred in the classroom happened because of them and not simply because of what the teacher said or did.

Because students set course priorities, the curriculum of Personal Growth Education will differ somewhat from group to group. In one group, more emphasis will be placed on nutrition and meal planning and on managing one's money, while in another group, making better use of leisure time and learning basic etiquette and what is and is not acceptable interpersonal behavior will receive more emphasis. Each course, however, covers all of these areas to greater or lesser degrees, taking into account both student priorities and the fact that, in any given area, one group may need to start at the most elementary level possible, while another may be able to start at a somewhat more advanced level.

From Patient to Student. One of the most important aspects of this course is that the students are called "students," see themselves as students, and have the identity of students. The teacher is not a mental health professional, and the setting is an educational one, not a mental health one, so long-term patients begin to see that they can be like other people in the community, doing things that other people do, such as going to school. When they meet people and are asked what they are doing, many of the students say, "I am going to school," or "I am taking a class in personal growth education." The prospect of returning to school also creates some apprehension at first, for many long-term patients have had previous negative experiences with the educational system or lack confidence in their ability to meet the demands of an educational setting. However, when they get there and find that the course is relevant to their needs and that they can handle it, their self-esteem is enhanced and they feel more secure in their ability to handle the demands of the world.

The course also helps long-term patients realize that the basic skills of everyday living are learned skills and not abilities or talents magically bestowed on others but not on them. Many long-term patients seem to have a fantasy that they are different from other people, that other people have acquired these skills in some unknown way. The students discover that others have also had to learn these skills, though perhaps in a different framework, that these are not skills that one is born with. Much of the mystique of coping with the world is taken away, and the students learn that they too can acquire the ability to "make it."

Classes are held four hours a day (with breaks excluded, a little over three hours of actual class time) two days a week, and the course lasts a full semester. The full course is offered twice a year, and a briefer summer session also is offered. Some students are allowed to repeat the course if they request it and the teacher feels it is appropriate. The small class size of ten to twelve people is a key factor. It gives the teacher a chance to know his students well, which is extremely important in learning how to help each student individually. Further, the small group allows for much interaction with fellow students. For instance, when budgeting is studied, each student draws up a budget and then the class discusses it. This technique is supportive in that all the students are going through the experience together. Furthermore, there is an opportunity for much give-and-take in what quickly becomes a close-knit group, and the students get feedback from one another in terms of what they did right, what they did wrong, and where they can improve.

The topic of budgeting also provides an example of how the practical results of some aspects of the course can be evaluated. After the classes where each student draws up a budget, continued class discussions provide the opportunity to observe how the students do over the remainder of the month and the following months. For many students, reaching the end of the month with a few dollars left is a new experience. In view of the fact that most students receive Supplemental Security Income (SSI) and that those students living in residential care facilities may have less than thirty-five dollars per month for all of their personal needs, this accomplishment is one that any of us would find impressive. Similarly, in the ongoing discussions following the classes on nutrition, meal planning, and shopping, the teacher gets a clear picture of what changes, if any, are taking place in the students' eating habits. Feedback from therapists indicates that the course has been especially helpful for persons moving from hospitals, halfway houses and residential care facilities to independent living situations.

Initial reactions to the course are frequently revealing regarding what the students have become used to in mental health settings and how they have to shift gears in moving to an educational setting. For instance, in drawing up the needs list, many of the students will at first request sightseeing trips, such as going to see an architecturally unique new hotel that has just been built or taking outings to the park. They have to adjust to a setting where what they are doing must be purposeful and part of the educational process. Though many of the students have spent years in mental health settings where they have become overly dependent, most are able to make the transition during the first few weeks—perhaps because many students have a deep need for purposeful activity. Students tell us later that they are sick of sightseeing trips and often requested such excursions simply because they felt that these requests fit the pattern expected of them.

The transition presents some problems for mental health professionals too. For instance, when Personal Growth Education was set up, a referral form was designed with room for past history, type of living situation, and comments by the therapist. At the bottom of the form was a release of information that the prospective student signed so that his therapist could give this information to the teacher. We now see that this procedure evolved from our own discomfort in operating outside of a mental health setting. Now, while therapists are encouraged to suggest to their patients that they take this course, the students simply report to the course and fill in the brief personal information form themselves. The original procedure was not only unnecessary, but made the student feel he was involved in yet another mental health setting. Occasions will, of course, arise when the teacher feels the need to talk to parents or other significant persons in the student's life. In such a situation, the teacher asks the student's permission and, if he wishes to talk with the therapist, he obtains a release of information that allows the therapist to talk with him about the student. This is done, however, as infrequently as possible.

After initial negotiations and organization of the course, this project costs the local mental health program nothing more than an average of one and one-half hours per week of the time of a mental health professional. For the student, the cost is two dollars for the registration fee. Courses such as this one compensate for the ego deficits and experiential lacks of long-term patients. They serve as an example of how to reintegrate the long-term patient at minimum cost to community mental health programs, if they are taught as classes, by teachers, and outside of a mental health setting. In these times of scarce mental health funds, we must look for new ways of involving other service systems in bringing needed services to long-term patients.

The Personal Growth Education teacher has easy access to and uses mental health consultation. But the course is his. And when he feels the need for resource people, they are persons from outside the mental health field, such as a home economics teacher (meal planning), a police captain (understanding the functions of the police), or a librarian (how to use the library). An incidental benefit of the class is that the student receives credit toward his high school diploma if he does not already have one. But, more importantly, the student has acquired a new identity, that of student, and feels that he can participate in activities outside of mental health centers, just like other people in the community. That identity, combined with the information imparted in the course, helps the student to move beyond the mental health system.

Using Recreation Departments and Libraries

Many mental health centers are increasingly making use of still other existing facilities within their own communities. They have found recreation departments and libraries receptive to the initiation of programs for long-term patients. Recreation departments have set up a variety of athletic activities, classes in sewing, needlepoint, and macrame, and also photography clubs specifically for long-term patients. Sometimes these are jointly led by mental health professionals and members of the recreation department staff. The more desirable programs, however, are those run solely by recreation department personnel, with only consultation from

mental health personnel. For many long-term patients, these activities can be transitional in the sense of being stepping stones to
the regular activities of the recreation department in which members of the general public participate. In order to facilitate this
transition, programs designed for the general public should make
special efforts to help hesitant persons coming alone feel welcome. I
might add that such efforts are important for many persons in the
community who are not long-term patients.

The public library can also be a rich resource. Many
librarians are extremely adept at leading literary discussion and
current events groups for long-term patients. Again, mental health
consultation to the library staff is important to the success of these
programs.

Friendship Centers

A concept that has been effective in helping long-term patients acquire social competence is that of the friendship center,
sometimes called a "friendship club" or "friendship circle." The
friendship center is staffed by volunteers and often is sponsored by
the local mental health association. Its purpose is to bring long-
term patients together under circumstances in which they can interact with one another and with "normal" members of the community—namely, the volunteers. It is hoped that the center decreases the isolation of these patients and helps them to increase
their social skills and their comfort in social situations. Another
goal is helping members learn how to use their leisure time, with the
hope that there will be a carry-over effect and the members will
increase their social interaction and use of community resources
outside of this program. The usual pattern is for the center to hold
meetings once a week for about half a day, often from 10 A.M. to
2 P.M. and usually in a church. The meetings center around social
and recreational activities. In a typical program, mornings are set
aside for such activities as crafts, table games, cooking, listening to
music, and just visiting. Lunch is a "brown bag" affair, except on
special occasions, when everyone participates in a potluck lunch.
Business meetings, with a chairman elected each month from the
group, follow lunch. These are important to increase group cohesiveness and to help the members become more active in planning their

activities and making decisions about their center. Afternoons are devoted to group activities, planned at previous meetings. These include outings such as a trip to the park for a picnic or a nature walk and trips to the county fair and various local tourist attractions. A key element in the concept of friendship centers is that they be staffed entirely by volunteers. Mental health professionals usually serve as consultants, but do not participate in the program itself.

Experience has shown that a paid coordinator of volunteers is essential, especially if the sponsoring agency contemplates a network of several centers. The coordinator need not be, and usually is not, a mental health professional. This person should have skills in community organization, an ability to communicate enthusiasm, and a willingness to be supportive to the volunteers when they feel anxious about a situation in the center.

The volunteers are recruited by the mental health association and for the most part are housewives, although occasionally there are male volunteers. Sometimes the church at which meetings are held becomes very involved in sponsoring or cosponsoring the program, in which case a large proportion of the volunteers may be members of the church. The volunteers must be carefully screened by the coordinator, perhaps with the assistance of the mental health consultant, so that the persons selected have the interpersonal skills necessary to work with long-term psychiatric patients. It is usually possible to obtain publicity through local newspapers and church bulletins to attract volunteers.

About once a month, after the friendship center closes, there is a meeting of all the volunteers from that center to discuss how the center is going, how to further increase community involvement, various problems with the members that have come up during the month, how they were handled, and alternative ways they might have been handled. The consultant usually attends this meeting. Each center has a volunteer chairman who presides over the monthly meeting and is generally the person in charge while the center is open.

Practical Consultation to Volunteers. It is essential to have a training program before volunteers begin working in a center. Most training is handled by the mental health consultant in conjunction with the coordinator. The training program need not be extensive, but it should include orientation to the various mental health facilities and programs in the community and should cover some of the rudiments of working with persons with emotional problems.

It is very helpful for the volunteers to understand the mental health system. This does not mean an in-depth understanding of the community mental health program, but rather knowledge of what a day treatment center is, what a sheltered workshop is, what a mental health clinic does, and how one manages to gain admission to these facilities. These facilities comprise a large part of the members' world, and the volunteer needs to understand what the members are talking about. At times, when a member is having a particular problem, the volunteer can help that person take advantage of these services. For instance, she might say, "I think that you should get some help with that problem at the clinic."

The mental health consultant performs an essential function by helping friendship center volunteers handle the everyday problems that arise in relating to long-term patients. These problems loom extremely large for volunteers, who, without guidance and support, feel insecure and anxious and frequently flee to a "less threatening" volunteer activity. For instance, the volunteer in a friendship center wonders what her degree of responsibility is if a member runs away. A simple statement from the consultant that the volunteer's responsibility is to work in the center and does not include being certain that members remain on the premises can be very reassuring. Further, the consultant lessens the volunteer's sense of guilt ("It's my fault that he ran away"), which otherwise might be overwhelming and drive the volunteer away. The same is true for the volunteer's concern about what her responsibility is if a member purposely harms himself. Again, the volunteers are helping to run an activity center; but they cannot take responsibility for controlling or stopping grossly pathological behavior, and they need to know this. If the member's behavior is grossly inappropriate or out of control, the volunteers should feel free to call a responsible person such as a parent, a spouse, or an operator of a residential care facility to come and get the member, and they also should feel that they may refuse to take him back until he can behave more appropriately.

The question of how to motivate members in a friendship

center will frequently leave volunteers in a quandry. Here the consultant can be helpful by encouraging one-to-one contact when necessary and by helping the volunteers understand that some members simply do not have the capacity at first to participate on their own. The volunteers can be most helpful in such cases by approaching the member and taking the initiative. Peer pressure is another effective way of motivating the members to engage not only in small-group activities such as arts and crafts but also in large-group activities such as cleanup. The volunteers need to understand that many groups of long-term patients will be reluctant to exert peer pressure on their fellow members. Encouraging peer pressure is often an important technique for the volunteer.

Many volunteers ask how to recognize progress in a member. Sometimes they are expecting too much too soon from long-term patients. The volunteer needs to understand that for many members, just being able to leave their residential care facilities or their families and come to the center at all is an accomplishment.

Probably nothing is more difficult for volunteers than feeling comfortable in being direct with members and setting limits on inappropriate behavior and unreasonable demands. The volunteer often assumes that mentally ill persons are very fragile and that saying no to them will cause them to fall apart. Typically, in such a situation, the volunteer becomes anxious and asks, "What should I do? I don't want to hurt him." Here the consultant's role is to help the volunteer feel free to say no to members' requests for personal information about the volunteer or to borrow money. And the volunteer needs to understand that not only will telling a member to stop inappropriate behavior frequently result in his becoming more appropriate, but it is helpful to the member in terms of improving his reality testing and his sense of what is socially acceptable. For example, the volunteer says to the consultant, "I just saw Joe steal the coffee money. What should I do?" It is very helpful when the consultant says, "Be direct. Tell him that you saw him take it and to put it back. He won't fall apart."

Drop-in Social Centers

Sometimes we in mental health seem to feel that patients spring into existence during working hours and go to some never-

never land in between. We pay too little attention to how the long weekend and evening hours are spent. For most of us, evenings and weekends are among our most satisfying times, but for the long-term patient with few resources and even fewer contacts, these are the really depressing and upsetting times. The drop-in social center is designed to meet these "after hours" needs of long-term patients.

Such a center, like the friendship center, should be staffed by volunteers and should not be located in a community mental health center or hospital. It can be organized and sponsored by the local mental health association or some other private, nonprofit agency. And, as in the case of the friendship center, a paid coordinator is crucial. The center need not operate twenty-four hours a day, but it is most important that it be open evenings and weekends. The drop-in center is a place where patients can come to talk or to play table games such as Ping-Pong. The atmosphere is informal—comfortable furniture, a coffee pot always going, a minimum of rules. Although one of the primary goals is to promote socialization, patients are free to choose their own levels of interaction. If a person simply wants to listen to music or read the newspaper and magazines that are available, the center still is providing a service that is important to that person; it must be remembered that long-term patients may feel lonely and have a need to be with people, but may, at the same time, maintain social distance, at least at first. Although the center should be staffed by volunteers, mental health professionals should be involved as consultants, and a professional should be on call whenever the center is open.

Unfortunately, drop-in social centers have a tendency to grow and expand in ways that defeat their primary purpose of being small, informal, noninstitutional gathering places. For instance, the drop-in social center should not become a treatment center. The informal, in-the-community atmosphere is lost if the center becomes a place where the person also receives therapy and medications. The center must not become professionalized. The entire character of such a center changes when professionals take over. Also, the center must guard against falling victim to the "edifice complex," with larger and larger and more and more expensive buildings. Along with such structures comes the need to justify them with additional programs.

Companion Programs

A number of communities have established programs based on prolonged one-to-one contact between volunteer and patient. As in the case of the friendship center, the volunteers are carefully selected and trained. The basic intent is to give the patient the experience of a warm, supportive relationship with a stable, well-adjusted member of the community—an experience that the patient sorely needs and may never have experienced. The program takes into account the needs of each patient and the personalities of the various patients and volunteers. Volunteers are then matched with patients on the basis of compatibility, in order to provide the best opportunity for a therapeutic result. In the program in Marin County, California, the volunteer makes a six-month commitment to the relationship; in other programs the commitment may be only three months. Frequently, however, by the time the formal commitment has ended, the relationship has turned into a mutual friendship and continues as such. The volunteer companion may spend anywhere from four to ten hours a week with the patient, depending on what is deemed appropriate and necessary. Some of the time is spent just talking, and some is spent going to various social and recreational activities. In some instances, and especially with more regressed patients, the companion provides help with transportation, shopping, and other daily-living activities. To the extent possible, public transportation is used, so that the patient does not regard the volunteer as a chauffeur. It is important that the patient see the volunteer as a person who does things with him, not for him; too much dependence on the companion is thus discouraged. As in the other programs described in this chapter, the long-term patient is given the opportunity to relate to someone who is not a patient or a mental health professional. It is hoped that the volunteer will provide a model for the patient in terms of coping and problem solving, acquiring social competence, and learning to use community resources.

The Marin County Companion Program initially gives its volunteers a three-week orientation, with six sessions of two to three hours each. To provide ongoing support, the two staff members make themselves available to the volunteers for consultation twenty-four hours a day. In addition, they hold evening group meetings once a week for two hours so that the volunteers can discuss problems they have encountered. Each volunteer is required to attend at least one group meeting every two weeks. The Marin County program has forty to sixty active volunteer companions at any given time.

Some companion programs also have as a goal providing enough support to those in crisis so that hospitalization or admission to a day treatment center can be averted. When this is the goal, the companions are much more highly trained, are considered paraprofessionals, and are paid. They may be with the patient in the patient's own living situation twenty-four hours a day until the crisis is past.

Community of Communities

In 1972, San Jose State University in California began a program called Community of Communities. This program uses college students to work on a day-to-day basis with the more than eleven hundred long-term psychiatric patients (and another six hundred alcoholics and drug abusers) who live in more than one hundred residential care facilities near the university (Moltzen, 1975). The students receive three units of college credit for participation in the program. Approximately two hundred students participate each semester. In the most recent one-year period, there were eighteen thousand hours of student service. Students are drawn from all departments of the university, not just those leading to entry into the helping professions. The program does not seek to provide treatment or therapy as such; rather, it focuses on organizing activities such as neighborhood cleanup days, street dances, trips to the beach, potluck dinners, picnics and Weight Watchers classes. Special activities are held to meet special needs of long-term patients. For instance, during the Christmas holidays, students hold an open house for them for four days from 10 A.M. to 10 P.M. Community of Communities publishes the *Street Journal,* a weekly neighborhood newsletter that is distributed to all of the county's residential care homes. Among its features is an entertainment and recreation calendar for the week.

The program philosophy is that normal activities bring about normal behavior. And, as we have seen in other settings, this philosophy works—sick behavior is dropped as the patients participate in normal community activities. Further, many of the patients have been brought out of their residential care facilities for the first time.

One overall purpose of the program is to facilitate interaction between the patients and their nonstudent neighbors. Both in the planned activities and informally, the students serve as a socially sanctioned medium of contact and interaction between the patients and their neighbors. Student activities are an accepted norm in this near-campus neighborhood. And the neighbors seem to feel, "If these untrained college students aren't fearful and hesitant to mingle with mental patients, why should I be?"

The students participating in Community of Communities have also become involved in efforts to protect the rights of long-term patients. They help patients deal with the Public Guardian, the Social Security office and the welfare department. They have gone to city council and planning commission meetings to urge that residential care homes be located in areas of the city other than that where the great majority of long-term patients are now concentrated. Toward this end, the students have succeeded in getting the city to adopt a policy that use permits not be required for homes with fewer than seven residents.

The Community of Communities program has met its objective of enriching the lives of long-term patients. It has enabled the patients to meet, and spend time with, "normal," enthusiastic college students. It also has been an excellent learning experience for the students.

Conclusions

Several common threads have run through this chapter. Long-term patients can best acquire social competence if their primary contact is with regular members of the community. They should spend as much time as possible in settings like those used by the community at large. Programs based on these premises— whether they are structured as courses taught by teachers, are friendship centers run by housewife volunteers, or are neighborhood activities organized by college students—all help integrate long-term patients into the community.

8

Victor Goertzel

Program
Evaluation

The 1960s witnessed the enactment of an unprecedented mass of legislation dealing with man's welfare. This legislation set up a wide variety of programs, most of which included a requirement that their worth be assessed. However, in their eagerness to implement new programs, funding sources often overlooked the evaluation requirement. Early enthusiasm was high, sometimes supported by evidence of success, sometimes not. Other factors entered in. For instance, the initial inspiration in pilot programs spurred staffs on to exceptional effort with the target populations, thus enhancing program effectiveness. As the years passed, yielding results frequently far below the earlier high expectations, routine and stagnation set in. Meanwhile, government and public, disenchanted with the results of human service programs so enthusiastically entered into, discovered that the cost of these programs was too high and, even worse, that they did not solve society's problems. The backlash of false hopes has been the tightening up of public funds. There is pressure to cut back existing programs and very strong resistance to initiating new proposals. Existing programs require extensive justification. There is pressure to save tax dollars. Government officials threaten to stop programs that do not generate data that justify their existence. Current discontent

130

with various crime control programs is illustrative. The combination of rising crime rates and rising law enforcement spending is a well-known phenomenon. The pressure for program evaluation nationwide has never been higher. And this comes at a time when there is finally recognition of the need to set up community services for long-term patients on a large scale basis.

Every program—national, regional, state, or local—needs to be objectively evaluated. Objectivity must be stressed, because without it we become dependent on our subjective impressions and are influenced by our biases. We remember that which fits in with our preconceptions and forget that which is in conflict with our beliefs (Goertzel, 1971). Most health and welfare workers feel that their work is important and has a positive influence on their clients. One of the purposes of scientific research methods is to minimize such subjective bias so that conclusions can be based on hard data. We know that every mental health professional, whatever his theoretical orientation and therapeutic methods, has some clients who improve and some who do not; no therapist is successful with all his patients. Therapists employ various treatment methods, depending upon the needs of various patients, but depending also upon their own preferences, orientations, and needs. Objective evaluation, however, can determine which methods are helpful for which therapists and with which clients, as well as whether the therapy itself has resulted in improvement. The study by Whitehorn and Betz (1975), more fully described in Chapter Two, is an excellent illustration of this point. They demonstrated that there is a very definite difference in the success rates of psychotherapy with schizophrenics depending upon the style and techniques of the therapist.

If an agency is to conduct program evaluation successfully a prerequisite is that there must be administrative support at all levels and willingness to undergo some inconvenience to facilitate the study. This seemingly obvious statement cannot be overemphasized; without firm and consistent administrative support, meaningful program evaluation cannot be accomplished.

Do community mental health centers collect the kind of data necessary to evaluate their effectiveness objectively? Unfortunately, the answer is usually no. Typically, what they do collect is such information as the number of patients treated and how long they stayed in treatment. Also included may be a rating of improvement at termination as compared with status at intake. These ratings are often determined perfunctorily and inconsistently by clinicians using poorly defined, subjective criteria. Such statistics are easy to collect and actually tell more about efficiency of operation than they do about effectiveness of treatment. The computerization of clinical records will make it even easier to gather such statistics than it is at present. Genuine evaluative research involves more than simply counting noses. It must develop some objective criteria for assessing patients' functioning outside of the treatment setting, and after treatment has stopped, and for assessing the effects of services upon those who received them.

Controlled Studies

An agency that seriously wants to evaluate its effectiveness must engage in controlled studies and run the risk of finding that its program, or some valued aspect of it, does not contribute to reaching stated objectives. This risk is particularly threatening to a prestigious agency that is generally satisfied with itself, with its reputation, and with its growth in terms of an increasing budget and the number of clients served. One might ask why such an agency would be motivated to evaluate its program, if it is so satisfied with itself. In an ideal world, the answer would be the universal craving for truth and knowledge. Unhappily, this craving is too often lacking. In most instances, such an agency undertakes an evaluation because it is certain that research will completely reinforce its conviction that its program is superior and will thus supply objective proof to the world of its superiority. Another factor that leads agencies into research efforts is that having a research program adds prestige, and not having one leaves the agency open to criticism and suspicion.

A controlled study is one in which a number of persons are not exposed to the program, or to that part of the program being evaluated, but are exposed to as many as possible of the other conditions in the study. These persons constitute the control group, as opposed to the experimental group that is exposed to the program being studied. The purpose is to ensure that the results under examination do not derive from experiences other than the one in question or from differences in the persons served. Thus, the control group should be comparable to the experimental group in all respects, including demographic factors (age, sex, education, race, social class), motivation, and psychiatric history, except that it is not exposed to the program being studied. Rigorously controlled studies, of course, can be conducted only in the laboratory, but they can be approximated in real life. It is possible to conduct a controlled evaluation by establishing a control group among the applicants who are denied service by the agency.

Comparable groups can be obtained by using some method of random assignment. Those applicants who meet the clearly defined requirements for eligibility for service can be assigned to the research groups by the use of a table of random numbers or strictly by rotation. If subjects are assigned to the experimental and control groups on a straight rotation basis—that is, if every second referral falls into the experimental group—the treatment staff can easily know which assignment is next and may manipulate the sequence of referrals to get patients assigned to whichever program the staff prefers in each case. Consequently, random assignment is preferable. If any system other than true randomization is used, clinicians may attempt to "beat the system" to get patients into the treatment they subjectively "know" is best for them. Prestudy and poststudy measurements should be obtained for all subjects, including members of the control group. Statistical tests should be made to determine that the groups do not differ with respect to demographic factors or in important psychiatric-history factors that might in themselves cause differences between the groups in the outcome of the study.

Mental health professionals show great reluctance to deny service to eligible applicants. They subjectively "know" their services are necessary, despite the lack of objective validation. They also fear that they will alienate referral sources by denying service for the purpose of research. But if they refuse to cooperate, then no one will ever really know whether the service is effective, or for whom.

The National Institute of Mental Health (NIMH) Collaborative Outpatient Study in Schizophrenia is an excellent example of an ongoing controlled study of the treatment of one major group of patients in the community (Hogarty and Goldberg, 1973; Hogarty, Goldberg, Schooler, and Ulrich, 1974). This study is a multiclinic attempt to show how two modes of treatment (drug and sociotherapy) interact in the prevention of relapse and the enhancement of community adjustment over a considerable period of time. The study design, criteria for case inclusion, and measurements used for evaluations were all carefully delineated (Hogarty, Goldberg, Schooler, and Ulrich, 1974, p. 603):

> Following discharge from three Maryland state hospitals, schizophrenic patients from Baltimore were randomly assigned at clinic intake to major role therapy (MRT), a combination of intensive social casework and vocational rehabilitation counseling. All patients were stabilized on chlorpromazine treatment for two months and then randomly assigned identical-looking tablets of chlorpromazine (Thorazine) or placebo. The study required 120 patients from each of three clinics. Patients stratified by sex were randomly assigned to all possible combinations of drug-placebo and MRT-no MRT, creating the following four treatment groups: drug alone, drug plus MRT, placebo alone, placebo plus MRT. The study was conducted at three clinics for two purposes; to obtain a sizable sample within a reasonable amount of time and to enable us to examine the consistency of results across facilities. Relapse was defined as clinical deterioration of such magnitude that rehospitalization was imminent. About 75 percent of relapsed patients were actually rehospitalized.

The method and procedure for establishing the four experimental groups is quoted in some detail to show that the process is not a simple one. Similar care was given to the selection of cases for inclusion in the study and to the measurement and evaluation of outcome. As a result of this study, it was concluded that chlorpromazine is significantly more effective than placebo in forestalling relapses. Within twenty-four months, 80 percent of placebo-treated patients had relapsed, compared to 48 percent of those treated with the drug. There was no statistically significant effect of MRT during the entire treatment period. However, sociotherapy does reduce relapses among those who survive in the community for six months after hospital discharge. Considerable confidence can be placed in these findings, as they were replicated at all three clinics.

The third paper from the NIMH Collaborative Outpatient Study in Schizophrenia examines the effects of drug and socio-therapy on the quality of community adjustment of patients remaining in the community during a two-year period following hospital discharge (Hogarty, Goldberg, and Schooler, 1974). The study found that persons treated with both a drug and sociotherapy adjust better than those taking the drug alone. The conclusion was that maximum restorative benefits require both maintenance pheno-thiazine and psychological treatment, continued for the full two years following hospital discharge. The important conclusions of the NIMH study could not have been reached if it had not been a controlled study.

Measures of Effectiveness

Evaluative research that has determined the effectiveness with which a program serves its particular clients still has not done enough. Effort must be directed toward objectively examining the overall efficacy of the program. The research must examine not only how well clients are served but also how great a contribution the program makes to solving a particular social problem, to meeting a particular need. For example, one social problem is the need for sheltered housing for patients returning from mental hospitals to the community. A halfway house may serve two such persons a month out of the twenty who return to the community. If, on the average, one of these clients per month moves into an independent living situation, the agency shows a superficially impressive 50 per-cent success rate, but it is actually making only a 5 percent (one in twenty) contribution to meeting the housing needs of all the mental hospital patients who return to the community during this period.

Community agencies and institutions must be aware of what people they are including for, or excluding from, service. The fund-ing agencies should require service agencies to report on the psy-chiatric, educational, economic, and other characteristics of the people who apply to, complete, and benefit from their programs. A clear statement should be made of what specific population is being served, and some attempt should be made to describe the characteristics of that portion of the needy population not being served.

Program evaluation can focus on quality, process, or outcome. Each kind of evaluation has its own aims, strategies, and appropriate procedures; each results in different kinds of information; and each has its limitations and its usefulness. Outcome, however, what actually happens to the recipient of services, is clearly and by far the most important measure. Unfortunately, meaningful outcome data usually are not obtained. Moreover, quality and process are frequently confused with outcome, with the result that program evaluation does not really measure effectiveness.

Quality is what clinicians usually have in mind when they make an informal appraisal such as, "We have a good program," or "Our program is not what it should be." "Quality" refers to the degree to which a treatment approaches some preconceived, usually theoretical, ideal standard. Regretfully, treatment might conform to the ideal standard while the patient decompensates. In its extreme form, the problem with both quality and process evaluation is illustrated by the cliche "The operation was a success but the patient died." Process evaluation, as its name suggests, means evaluating the process by which the patient is treated and involves measurement, for example, of the movement of patients through the phases of a service. In a psychiatric outpatient clinic, process evaluation should include the time intervals between the first telephone referral by a social worker and the date of the first intake interview with the patient, between that interview and the dates of the psychological testing, and between the testing and the actual beginning of individual or group therapy.

Some measurement of outcome, of the effectiveness of services upon those served, is the sine qua non of program evaluation. However, outcome evaluation is not simple. Many factors other than treatment influence outcome. Hospital return rates were once regarded as really hard data, a clear index of treatment success or failure. A closer look, however, shows that return rates may be an incomplete measure of outcome. For example, ex-patients who felt that the original hospital treatment was ineffective may avoid going back to the hospital again or may seek alternative resources. Return to a hospital may be more closely related to the unwillingness of the family to put up with a troublesome family member than to the functioning level of the ex-patient. Or rehospitalization may be a temporary and therapeutic interlude in an ultimately successful rehabilitation program. Thus, what at first glance looks like a simple and important piece of hard data is not at all simple to interpret.

Meaningful outcome evaluation requires that the goals of a program be clearly formulated and defined and stated in operational terms that can be objectively measured. More will be said about this point below.

Exposure to multiple programs is another complication in outcome evaluation. When many resources are available for a particular target population, there is an inclination to shower programs upon the subjects. For example, a number of disadvantaged youths might be given a variety of programs with the goal of getting them into paying jobs. These programs could include class training, prevocational work experience, a sports and outing program, hot lunches, and a summer camp experience. Even if the desired change occurs and is measured, it is almost impossible to sort out the relative contributions of the different programs to the outcome. In the study by Hogarty, Goldberg, Schooler, and Ulrich (1974) referred to earlier in this chapter, the researchers were aware of the problem of exposure to multiple programs. Therefore, subjects were randomly assigned to all possible combinations of drug-placebo treatment and sociotherapy-no sociotherapy. This permitted evaluation of the effects of drug treatment alone and sociotherapy alone as well as the effect of both treatments combined.

Clarification of Goals

In some ways, the position of the clinician appears to be incompatible with that of the researcher. The clinician must have faith in the value of what he is doing and must convey this faith to the client. The researcher, on the other hand, approaches his task with a questioning attitude. He must be skeptical, dispassionate, and objective. But this apparent incompatibility should be seen in a different perspective. For instance, often there is lack of clarity within the agency with respect to the broadest aspects of treatment goals

—for example, should the goal be reduction of specific symptoms or insight, competitive employment or social rehabilitation? Further, as noted earlier, staffs frequently confuse process with outcome. The discussion between clinicians and program evaluators for the purpose of formulating criteria to be used in the planned study can lead to a clarification of the agency's goals.

This positive outcome of collaboration between clinicians and researchers is illustrated in a recent Veterans Administration study specifically designed to help day treatment center staffs define their goals (Schroeder, Davis, and others, 1975). The authors feel that defining goals is a necessary first step in program evaluation. The design of the study involved getting staff response to a questionnaire listing eight goals derived from an earlier, nationwide survey. The respondents were asked to rate the eight goals on a scale of 0 (not a goal of a day treatment center) to 6 (extremely important). In brief, after analysis of the data, agreement was obtained upon a list of goal statements that are outcomes rather than processes, that are patient-oriented rather than therapist-oriented, and that can be, to a relative extent, objectively evaluated. These goals are that, when leaving a day treatment center, the patient should be able to manage his own affairs without intensive supervision or treatment (such as is provided by a day treatment center); interact successfully with family members, peers, and authorities; achieve or strive for economic independence; avoid behavior that has or can have harmful consequences to himself or to others; perceive, remember, think, and judge accurately and efficiently; and maintain emotional equilibrium. Under each goal specific examples are listed. For instance, the goal of achieving or striving for economic independence has been met if the patient is working, looking for work if unemployed, or seeking training if currently unemployable.

With this list of goals and specific examples of each goal, a rating scale can be constructed that would make possible a meaningful and quantifiable outcome evaluation of day treatment center services.

The Treatment Process

Thus far we have presented some of the problems in evaluating programs and some of the means for making research more meaningful. What about gaining a better understanding of the relation between treatment and outcome? Do we know what really works? Is it the treatment method that determines outcome? Is it the relationship with a therapist? What makes a patient get better? Would he still improve if he were not in treatment at all? The thorny issue of the waiting list is a case in point.

A study by Saenger (1970) sheds light on this issue. He did a one-year-after-intake follow-up on more than a thousand patients, comparing those who had been treated to those who had remained on the waiting list. He presents evidence in his paper that psychiatric outpatient treatment helped patients with a poor prognosis—as compared to when such patients were left on a waiting list. In contrast, patients considered to have a good prognosis tended to improve more often when left on a waiting list than when treated. In the discussion of his findings, Saenger says that if further research with randomly assigned patients should substantiate these findings, it would suggest that clinics might be well advised to devote more of their efforts to those cases they tend to consider poor treatment risks rather than to patients with a good chance of recovery even without treatment. This point is especially important in the context of this book, in that long-term patients are usually included in the "poor treatment risk" category.

The "hello–good-bye" effect should not be overlooked. Patients may enter treatment at a time of crisis or a low point in a periodic illness and leave at a high point, with the therapist claiming that the difference is the result of his own intervention rather than a natural change in status. Again, controlled studies with objective, long-term follow-up procedures are necessary to draw meaningful conclusions.

The work of Eysenck (1952, 1969) is relevant to any discussion of the effects of psychotherapy. A quarter of a century ago, he systematically examined all the published evidence regarding the claims for psychotherapeutic effectiveness. He quotes statistics that justify the conclusion that with severely ill neurotics, spontaneous remission was an undoubted fact. Much further work has been published on this point since. For instance, Rachman (1972) reviewed the available evidence and confirmed Eysenck's estimate of a gross spontaneous remission rate of approximately 65 percent of neurotic disorders over a two-year period. Rachman emphasizes the need for more refined studies to analyze the spontaneous remission rates of neurotic patients with particular types of disorders. We should not overlook the fact, however, that approximately one third of all neurotic patients do not improve spontaneously. It is hoped that, in these times of scarce mental health dollars, these neurotics, along with long-term disabled schizophrenics, are the people who will absorb the attention of clinicians and researchers.

Meaningful Evaluation

The obvious reason for conducting evaluation studies is to get objective information that can be used by the agency being studied and by other agencies as a guide for program development. The chances of research findings being used are enhanced if three conditions prevail: the staff is actively involved in the study; research is initiated in response to the agency's felt need; and research findings are rapidly reported. It is most important that the staff be involved in all phases of the study, from its beginning to its completion, including the formulation of the specific questions to be answered, the data-gathering phase, and the interpretation of the meaning and the implications of the results. Only in this way does the staff feel that it has a stake in the research and cooperate fully. Because of staff turnover, this process of sustaining interest and involvement is a continuous one. Time must be taken to inform new staff members of the history and current status of the research. Without the cooperation of the staff, it is impossible for the researcher to obtain the material he needs. Therefore, throughout the study, the researcher must inform the clinical staff of what he is doing and why he is doing it.

The type of study most likely to be used in program development is one made in response to an immediate felt need of the agency. The study may be, for example, a rapid initial project aimed at helping to solve an acute crisis. Clinical decisions often must be made quickly, based on data the researcher feels are inadequate in terms of statistical significance. This use of "dirty data" is among those issues upon which the following examples of a controlled study sheds some light. The study was conducted by Lamb and

Goertzel (1974, 1975). It illustrates the use of a controlled study to give a true picture of the overall effectiveness of a new social program, the importance of prompt reporting of findings, and the use of "dirty data" to correct shortcomings in a service program.

Ellsworth House is a community rehabilitation program for adult offenders offering an alternative to incarceration within the regular jail system. Residents of the house are able to engage in competitive employment in the community while participating in a therapeutic program at the house. The project was conducted as a controlled study during its initial three years of grant funding. In this study, offenders already sentenced to the county jail for a term of four months or more were randomly assigned either to Ellsworth House or to a comparison group of offenders who remained in the jail system.

Early in the project, as the first six-month postrelease data came in, we could see that recidivism was much higher for the Ellsworth House group than for the comparison group, even though the small numbers involved prevented this data from being statistically significant. This kind of preliminary data, small numbers, which lack statistical significance, is often referred to as "dirty data." Dirty data, however, can be suggestive, and often crucial, for evaluation in the early stages of a project. Accordingly, we used these early tentative results as a signal that we should reexamine and scrutinize our program from top to bottom. And what we saw was extremely revealing. Initially, men who had graduated had been supervised primarily on a group basis, while the men in the comparison group received close one-to-one supervision from their probation officers. Furthermore, in our initial concern with setting up the program, we had involved the Ellsworth House probation officer extensively in helping with the in-house program, thereby reducing the amount of time he could spend on follow-up with released offenders. The Ellsworth House graduates clearly needed more support and structure; at this point we freed the probation officer's time to allow for intensive individual follow-up supervision and, toward the same end, added a second probation officer to the program.

It also became clear to us that there had been a hesitancy on the part of our rehabilitation-oriented staff to set adequate disciplinary limits for the offenders. In their efforts to be "therapeutic," some of the staff had lost sight of the behavior-modification aspects of the program, namely the need to reward an individual's positive efforts to change his life-style and to punish or at least not reward the opposite. Steps were taken to remedy this laxness, including efforts to prevent drug use by giving unannounced urinalyses to residents at random times and whenever there was any suspicion of such behavior. The probation officer placed more emphasis on verifying that residents were employed or attending college or training programs, and he also increased his unannounced visits to the residents' places of employment or training. His stricter supervision greatly decreased the number of men who said they were leaving the house during the day for employment but were in fact spending time in the community with their former delinquent associates. Even more important, the staff and the residents began spending more time working together to identify specific time-limited goals for each resident, so that he would not simply drift through the program without being affected by it. Such goals included vocational planning to increase job satisfaction and work adjustment, resolution of family problems, learning how to make satisfying use of leisure time, finding new friends who do not have a delinquent orientation, and, if indicated, becoming involved in psychotherapy. In the process, the staff members began to look more closely at themselves and their own actions, which tended to defeat the behavior modification aspects of the program. They were thus forced to recognize their ambivalence about setting limits and imposing appropriate penalties for antisocial behavior.

The results of this evaluation and program change were dramatic. Recidivism in the Ellsworth House group immediately dropped to the level for the comparison group, and the levels have remained similar to the present time. If there had not been a comparison group, the recidivism rate might well have been ignored and attention focused instead on "success stories" and the high rate of employment. As it was, conducting the community rehabilitation program within a controlled research framework forced attention to be focused on a program deficiency and resulted in a dramatic improvement in program practices.

When one- and two-year follow-ups became available, it was clear that the rate of recidivism for the experimental group was not significantly different from that for the control group. This finding meant a rethinking of the goals of the program. Originally, the hope and the expectation had been that the program not only would be a more humane one, but would decrease recidivism. Now, the program has been continued even after the federal grant has ended, but with less ambitious goals and without a control group; regardless of its inability to lower recidivism rates, it is valued as a more humane program that allows a man to work in the community while incarcerated and does not completely remove him from his family.

A Controlled Demonstration Project

We have seen that most programs in mental health and rehabilitation are not evaluated in a scientific way. We have emphasized the need, in conducting research, for administrative support at all levels and for controlled studies. We have noted some of the problems associated with doing such studies—problems in making research meaningful and useful. But despite all the problems, programs can be meaningfully evaluated.

At the Mendota Mental Health Institute in Madison, Wisconsin, there is currently in progress a well-controlled study that deserves attention (Stein, Test, and Marx, 1975). It is a clinical research program that is a radical departure from the prevailing system for treating severely disturbed patients, namely short-term hospitalization plus aftercare. The program's approach is based on the assumption that deficiencies in coping skills and aggressive dependency are primarily responsible for high readmission rates to mental hospitals and that coping skills and autonomy are best learned in the community, where the patient will be needing and using them.

The subjects are all patients seeking admission for inpatient care at the Institute. They live in one particular county, are between eighteen and sixty-two years of age and have any diagnosis other than severe organic brain syndrome or primary alcoholism. Eligible subjects are randomly assigned to either the community treatment or the control group. Control patients are treated in the hospital as long as necessary and then linked with appropriate community agencies. Experimental patients do not enter the hospital, but are treated according to the "training in community living" approach for fourteen months. Assessment data on all subjects are gathered at admission and every four months for thirty-six months by a research staff that is independent of both clinical teams.

Patients assigned to the control group are usually, although not necessarily, admitted to the hospital, where they receive progressive treatment aimed at return to the community. They are all housed in one unit, which serves the county from which they come. This unit serves as a stringent control for the experimental program, because it has a high staff-to-patient ratio and offers a wide variety of services, including inpatient treatment, partial hospitalization, and outpatient follow-up. It is by no means a custodial unit; its median length of stay is only seventeen days, and it makes extensive use of the aftercare services available in Madison for discharged patients.

The community treatment approach focuses directly on an in vivo teaching of coping skills as well as on treating the acute problem that precipitated the patient's coming to the hospital. A complete hospital-ward staff (psychiatrist, psychologist, social worker, occupational therapist, nurses and aides) was retrained for community work. Staff are "on the spot" in patients' homes and neighborhoods—at places of work, supermarkets, and recreational facilities. They become involved in such fundamental, ordinary daily activities as shopping, cooking, laundry, grooming, budgeting, using transportation, and going to restaurants. Patients are helped to use leisure time constructively and to develop effective social skills by staff members' prodding and supporting their involvement in relevant community recreation and social activities.

The community was carefully prepared for the implementation of the experimental treatment program through a pilot study (Marx, Test, and Stein, 1973) in which conferences were held with every relevant community agency. Influencing them to respond to patients in a manner that would promote responsible behavior rather than reinforce maladaptive modes of coping with stress was a major goal. Sometimes, conferences alone were insufficient. It was found, for example, that though the workshop administration had given its support, daily contact with floor supervisors was necessary. Staff members were made available on an around-the-clock basis for crisis intervention.

The measures used are a symptomatology rating scale, a community adjustment form, and a "family burden" scale. The results at one-year follow-up strongly suggest that such a program can successfully treat patients with a high level of symptomatology (Test and Stein, 1975). Not only was hospital stay dramatically reduced, but patients showed a high level of community functioning. Further, there was a significant decrease in the burden felt by families of experimental patients. Most importantly, because there is a true control group, we know that these are significant findings.

The early report of the Mendota Institute study is an encouraging demonstration of the feasibility of a training-in-community-living program for patients who would otherwise be treated in public mental hospitals. A cost-benefit analysis is part of the research. It is hoped that later follow-up data will show that this program also has enhanced the long-term community adjustment of its patients, as compared to the control group.

How do we evaluate the success of a demonstration project? There are at least two levels at which this can be done. The first level is how well does the project work? There is every indication that the project at Mendota works, at least in the short run. The second level is the extent to which the project continues to be used after the demonstration has been completed. It is naïve to believe that if a model works successfully, it automatically will be adopted. The Mendota project required an earlier pilot project to prepare the community to work with patients. It is supported by a Hospital Improvement Program grant from the National Institute of Mental Health. It required considerable retraining of professional staff. As the researchers recognize, it required a "transition from work in a highly structured hospital setting, where little is required in the way of individual decision making, to work in the inevitably unstructured setting of the community, where a great deal of initiative and willingness to make decisions on the spot is vital" (Stein, Test, and Marx, 1975, p. 518).

The true tests of such projects come when grants run out and staffs are no longer working within a controlled research framework in which outcomes are objectively evaluated. Then there is a tendency to return to traditional ways. Further, how many other hospitals and institutes will, for example, do the work required to prepare the community and retrain the staff in order to substitute a training-in-community-living approach as an alternative to the prevailing system of short-term hospitalization plus aftercare?

Conclusions

In recent years, as pressure for determining the worth of social programs has increased, program evaluation has received a great amount of verbal support. Everybody talks about it, but few people are doing anything about it. We have stated that, ideally, evaluations should be conducted within a controlled research framework. At a minimum, program goals must be explicit and formulated in a manner that permits objective evaluation of the program. We must be prepared to terminate programs that do not produce evidence of their worth. Perhaps in this way mental health professionals can regain the high level of confidence and respect once given them by government and the general public. It is crucial that the general disenchantment with social programs not be allowed to impede the development of the community programs that are beginning to emerge for long-term patients.

9

Priscilla Allen

A Bill of Rights
for Citizens Using
Outpatient Mental
Health Services

What am I doing here? How did I, a "former mental patient now living in the community," find a place in this book written by mental health professionals? The agent that brought us all together is the Bill of Consumer, Tenant, and Human Rights for Citizens Using Outpatient Mental Health Services, which I authored.

When I identify myself as a "former patient" I am, in a sense, negating the central thesis of this book, the thesis that states: We who have been patients must again learn to see ourselves in other roles (students, workers, artists, lovers, whomever). However, in these particular circumstances, my identity as an ex-patient is central to the task we are undertaking. That task is to become familiar with the rights of consumers of mental health services. And consumers of mental health services are, of course, patients or clients. Moreover, the bill of rights, as I have formulated it, is inextricably linked with my own experiences as a patient. The goal of this bill

147

of rights is to assist patients in finding their way toward the status of full citizenship. And that is the goal toward which the authors of this book also address their efforts.

Since I shall be talking about the problems of patients, I want the reader to know that my credentials are among the best in respect to this area of human inquiry. I sometimes say that I am the possessor of three academic degrees: a B.A. in humanities from a university; an M.I. (Mental Illness) awarded after two years of rigorous experiential learning at one of California's state mental hospitals; and a B.C. (Board and Care) that followed two more years of applied study as a resident of a board and care home in San Francisco. Because mental illness is in no way a joke, I am somewhat uncomfortable with this rather facetious manner of summarizing my experiences. However, this list of "academic degrees" does give you, quickly and succinctly, a pretty good idea of where I have been! And, incidentally, it should place me in good stead with the other authors of this book, for have I not identified myself in exactly the same way that many "normal" people do—by placing a series of initials after my name? How much more "normal" can one get?

When and Where Was this Bill of Rights Developed?

In late 1972, I was discharged from a state hospital to live in a San Francisco board and care home, now called a "residential care facility." There I endured the stifling atmosphere that frequently prevails in such environments. This is an atmosphere that is characterized, for the most part, by silence, occasional small talk, and apparently meaningless noise. My first attempt to break through the unstated but consistently enforced prohibition against free speech consisted of written testimony that I submitted in July, 1973, to the California Senate Select Committee on Proposed Phaseout of State Hospital Services (the Alquist Committee). This testimony was later published as an article in *The Psychiatric Quarterly* under the title "A Consumer's View of California's Mental Health Care System" (Allen, 1974b).

In the article, I stress, among other points, that many patients "living in the community" can hardly be said to be living in the community at all; that community facilities such as board and care homes are often as effective, if not more effective, in institutionalizing patients as are state hospitals; that, in my opinion, for specific types of patients, state mental hospitals will be for the foreseeable future a necessary treatment resource. I also recommend that more professionally trained staff, and volunteers working under professional supervision, be available to assist the administrators and residents of residential care facilities.

Approximately seven months after I submitted the Alquist Committee testimony referred to above, I began to develop additional concerns. By March 1974, I was becoming more acutely aware of the fact that increased staffing (whether by professionals or by volunteer workers) might solve some problems but could well create others. I realized, to a sometimes alarming extent, that those who come to "help" are not always helpful. Whereas previously I had worried about the neglect to which long-term patients are subjected (and I continue to worry about this neglect, this nonobservance of the right to treatment), I now turned my attention to the abuses that can be perpetrated in the name of "treatment" (that is, to the need for a right to refuse treatment). I began thinking, too, about the right to confidentiality of personal records; the need for appropriate protection of one's economic rights; the client's rights as a rent-paying tenant; civil rights inherent in being a citizen; and the all-embracing and very important right to information, the right to be informed about matters vital to one's personal well-being.

Simultaneously, I read a recommendation published by the Citizens Advisory Council, a group mandated by state law (in sections of the California Welfare and Institutions Code) to advise the California Director of Health on mental health issues. The council was calling for a bill of rights very similar to the one that was taking shape in my mind, and their recommendation strengthened my own convictions. It was in March 1974, then, that I began to set down on paper my formulation of what I thought a bill of rights for community people using outpatient mental health services ought to be.

How was the Bill of Rights Written?

There are two factors pertaining to the manner in which this bill of rights was written to which I should like to call the reader's attention.

First, this document was indeed written with blood, sweat, and tears—and with considerable fear and trepidation added for good measure. To write a bill of rights in an atmosphere where *the right to have any rights at all* is not recognized is a terrifying experience. The atmosphere in most board and care homes is autocratic to the extreme. To think free thoughts is to practice heresy. In addition, intrapsychic prohibitions and censorships supported, or were supported by, the message I was receiving from the environment. Thus, for every single right that I set down on paper, I had to battle against and conquer the feeling that I had no right to be writing anything. The final result of this personal struggle was that my feelings and attitudes changed to the extent that I no longer fitted into the life-style of the board and care home. In early 1975 it became necessary for me to move to a San Francisco residence club.

Initially, the items that I set down in the bill of rights came from the lessons of my own experience. These lessons were later supplemented by material from the Mental Health Law Project of Washington, D.C., and other sources. But whatever the origin of each right, formulation always precipitated the same struggle: "Dare I say this?" "Yes." . . . "No." . . . And finally, "Yes!"

The second point I want to emphasize about the writing of this bill of rights is that the specific rights listed are included because they need to be included. To a person who lives in the "normal world," some of these rights may seem self-evident or in the nature of "that which can be taken for granted in any civilized environment." But herein lies one key to understanding the deficiencies of community treatment in general and of board and care home resources specifically. It is precisely the needs that "anyone would take for granted" that are commonly neglected. And that is one of the reasons why these needs continue, year after year, to be neglected —because no one would think that they could possibly be ignored!

Please allow me to give one example. Many people are probably aware that treatment and efforts toward rehabilitation are sparse in residential care facilities. But most people assume that clients are, as a basic minimum, adequately housed and fed. Not so! Housed? The roof leaks; wind and rain blow in through cracks around the windows; heating is often inadequate; safety hazards, such as loose linoleum, are usually more numerous than are efforts to repair them. (And if all of these specific conditions do not exist in any one home, other comparable indications of neglect are likely to be encountered.) Fed? Please read the section of the bill of rights pertaining to food. Clients grow obese (from excessive fats and starches)' while simultaneously suffering from malnutrition, possible high cholesterol levels, and other unhealthy conditions. Hygiene and sanitation? After meals, partially full bowls of soup are often dumped back into the cooking pot; plates returned to the kitchen are scraped into storage containers instead of into the garbage, so the food can be re-served at a future meal. And this pattern extends to the area of treatment, too, where errors in administering medication are not infrequent.

I would hesitate to make statements such as the above on the basis of only my personal experience (living in one board and care home and visiting nine others in connection with a survey I made before selecting one home as my personal residence). However, my evaluations so closely parallel those which have been well-documented by Congressional investigations of nursing homes that they would be difficult to dispute. Board and care home and nursing home situations are very similar. Those who are weak or powerless, whether because of age or because of mental or emotional disability, are easily exploited, and there is small chance that persons in positions of responsibility will insist on remedial action.

Another consideration that might cause me to question my evaluations of residential care living is the nature of the comments made by many people who live in these homes. When asked how they like their living conditions, most will say, "It's nice," or, "I like it fine." I found this to be the customary response when I, still a state hospital patient, visited those nine board and care homes for the survey I was making. Especially in reply to inquiries about such an important component of daily living as the quality of the food, I never once received a negative evaluation; and I was in some instances talking with acquaintances whom I had known in the hospital, people who might be inclined to speak quite candidly with me. Yet when I myself lived in one of these board and care homes, I found some of the food to be worse than anything I had ever been able to imagine. (Institutional meals look and taste like gourmet cooking in comparison.)

Why had my friends so misinformed me? Surely, as a "fellow patient," I had an "advantage" in winning their trust and eliciting frank responses. The sad fact is that even to a fellow patient, residents dare not speak the truth. Sometimes when they say, "It's nice," they are thinking, "in comparison to other board and care homes where I've lived." At other times they are observing the long-established rule that one is just not supposed to complain or protest as long as one resides within the residential care home system. And often, residents have remained silent so long that they no longer even think the truth to themselves. They have come to believe—or talked themselves into believing, in order to be able to tolerate the conditions that they must tolerate—that the way they are living is satisfactory. Furthermore, they have become convinced that this life is "the best they deserve."

But the above, rather lengthy digression into some of the details of residential care living was initially intended as an illustration of a factor that is central to the dynamics of the preparation of this bill of rights. As I indicated earlier, each right is included as a response to an observed human need—and usually a response to an observed abuse or neglect concerning that need as well. The rights enumerated in this bill are derived, not from a process of academic or legalistic theorizing, but from a direct, survival-oriented, personal struggle.

Where is this Bill of Rights Now, and Where is it Going?

It is my hope that the need for a bill of rights for consumers of outpatient mental health services will become more widely known and that the concepts that make up this bill will be studied and refined. In pursuit of that hope, I am happy to see this document find its way, through the medium of this book, to you, the reader. I hope that the needs to which the bill addresses itself will become, for you, matters of interest and serious concern.

A Bill of
Consumer, Tenant, and Human Rights
for Citizens Using
Outpatient Mental Health Services

Statement of Intent

Unless they are subject to specific legal limitations, persons living in the community utilizing mental health services on an outpatient basis are entitled to all the rights that ordinarily accompany citizenship. In fact, however, they are denied many of these rights. This Bill has been formulated in order to bring into sharper focus some of the areas where the greatest deficiencies in true citizenship are most frequently encountered.

In this Bill, specific means for enforcement of these rights have not been spelled out. Similarly, channels for appeal are not clearly delineated.

It is hoped, nonetheless, that the enumeration of these important rights will bring about an improved status for consumers of outpatient *mental health services in the community (as did significant legislation in many states, during recent years, for those persons* confined within *psychiatric facilities). Having been explicitly stated, these rights may be less easily ignored.*

Each consumer of public or private mental health services, living freely in the community (that is, any person who is not voluntarily or involuntarily a patient in a state, county, or private inpatient psychiatric facility—in which case the state or locally established rights for hospitalized patients shall apply[1]—and any

---

[1] In California, rights for patients confined in psychiatric facilities are enumerated in the California Welfare and Institutions Code, as revised in 1974, effective January 1975. The following rights (enumerated in Section 5325) "shall be prominently posted in English and Spanish in all facilities providing such services . . . :

"(a) To wear his own clothes; to keep and use his own personal

person who is not placed under other specific, legally established limitations) shall have the following consumer, tenant, and human rights, a list of which shall be prominently posted in English and whatever language is applicable in all facilities providing such services.

One: The Right to Voluntary Treatment and/or Services

Every client who desires such services shall have access to appropriate medical, psychiatric, psychological, psychosocial (resocialization, life-skills learning), residential, supportive, occupational, vocational, educational, cultural, and recreational resources. A full continuum of varying levels of integrated and coordinated services—from intensive care or treatment to occasional consultation—shall be available. Particular consideration shall be given to:

A. *Personalized Treatment and Services*

The term *personalized* means: first, that treatment and services are tailored to fit the client, instead of vice versa, and second, that the essential ingredient in treatment is not programs, plans, mechanisms and devices, but rather people—

---

possessions . . . ; and to keep and be allowed to spend a reasonable sum of his own money for canteen expenses and small purchases.

"(b) To have access to individual storage space for his private use.

"(c) To see visitors each day.

"(d) To have reasonable access to telephones, both to make and receive confidential calls.

"(e) To have ready access to letter writing materials, including stamps, and to mail and receive unopened correspondence.

"(f) To refuse shock treatment.

"(g) To refuse psychosurgery. . . .

"(h) Other rights, as specified by regulation."

Section 5326 states that "The professional person in charge of the facility or his designee may, for good cause [to be defined by regulations], deny a person any of the rights under Section 5325, except [the right to refuse psychosurgery, an absolute right] under subdivision (g), and the rights [to refuse shock treatment] under subdivision (f) may be denied only under the conditions specified in [a following section]." That section, number 5326.4. requires adherence to very strict, written informed consent and professional review procedures.

Denials of rights must be recorded. "Denial of a person's rights shall in all cases be entered into the person's treatment record" (Section 5326).

The code further provides that "any physician who violates" rights *the interactions of persons with other persons.* This is how treatment presents itself from the consumer's vantage point, and this is the aspect of treatment that must be emphasized in any statement on *human* rights.

1. Right to *qualified* staff in *numbers* sufficient to administer adequately the programs that are required to meet individual client needs. *Qualified staff* shall be considered to mean *trained, skilled, responsible* people who *care.*

2. Right to a personal evaluation of the client's problems, needs, assets, limitations, aspirations, and goals; with the *client's participation* and express and informed *consent,* development of a *flexible* treatment, rehabilitation, and/ or services plan directly suited to the client's needs; assignment of *responsibility* to specific people and agencies for being available to the client and for implementing this plan; periodic review and reevaluation, with continuing responsiveness to the client's direct or indirect communications and overall state of being.

3. Right to *orientation regarding his or her rights* (including both instruction on how to use appeal and complaint-

---

pertaining to psychosurgery or shock treatment "shall be subject to a civil penalty of not more than ten thousand dollars ($10,000) for each violation or revocation of license, or both." The attending physician who administers treatment in violation of rights pertaining to psychosurgery or shock treatment may also be held personally liable for damages in a civil action against the physician himself (Section 5326.5).

The history of patient rights legislation in California has been such that we are currently at a point of uncertainty and litigation. Rights (a) through (f) and right (h) were established in 1968 by the Lanterman-Petris-Short Act. This legislation also provided for the absolute right (g) to refuse lobotomy. It contained strict protection of privacy of personal records, with a five-hundred-dollar fine for breach of confidentiality. Indeterminate periods of commitment were replaced by strict time limitations: seventy-two hours, fourteen days, and so on, with the right to file a writ of habeas corpus after a period of seventy-two hours' evaluation.

The 1974 statutory amendments and additions (Chapter 1534) to the California Welfare and Institutions Code changed the right to refuse lobotomy to the right to refuse psychosurgery and established the informed consent and strict review procedures and penalties enumerated above. These amendments and additions are being tested in the courts. Their constitutionality is challenged on the grounds that they are restrictive to the degree that they infringe upon the right to treatment (shock treatment).

filing procedures and information about availability of client advocates) *as an integral part of the treatment and services plan.*

4. Right to *effective cooperation* between professionals and personnel of various facilities, especially between staffs of inpatient and outpatient services. *Before* a patient is discharged from inpatient status—particularly from a state hospital—he or she shall already be in touch with persons who can assist the client in his or her transition into the life of the community. State hospital–community liaison personnel shall be available to the client for this purpose.

5. Right to a system of record keeping that meets professional standards but consumes a minimum amount of staff time, thus allowing maximum staff resources for actual treatment and assistance to the client.

6. Right to treatment and services suited to the client's needs, *regardless* of age or degree of disability. No client shall be subject to neglect.

7. Right to see and confer regularly with a mental health professional whose training and character best qualify him or her to assist this particular client. Right to confer with a psychiatrist regularly, especially if the client is using medication prescribed for a psychiatric condition.

8. Right to be referred to a psychiatrist in private practice— for prescription of medication and/or individual psychotherapy—as provided under Medicaid (Medi-Cal in California).

9. Right to have a personal medical doctor and a personal dentist, and the services of other specialists as required.

10. Right to the services of a social worker, community care worker, or other qualified person to assist the client with problems of adjustment; to assure that the client receives appropriate and adequate followup care; to act as advocate on behalf of the client's interests; and to provide *continuity* of services by maintaining a long-term relationship with the client, if the client desires this type of assistance.

B. *Crisis Intervention*

Right to the services of *qualified and responsible* professional mental health workers, on twenty-four-hour call to visit the client at his residence for the purposes of averting, alleviating, and helping to resolve crisis situations. Recognizing the position of extreme vulnerability of a client in a crisis situation, it is necessary to emphasize that special efforts shall be made to protect the client's rights and to ensure that he or she maintains maximum autonomy and self-determination. The client shall be *informed* of his or her rights directly and explicitly. Most especially, the client shall be advised of his or her *right to refuse* treatment, including outpatient medication whether administered orally or by injection. The client shall be assured that he or she will be neither rewarded in any way, direct or indirect, for accepting treatment nor penalized or inconvenienced in any way, direct or indirect, for not accepting treatment. At no time shall medication or "treatment" be administered by a police officer or others who do not possess the necessary medical and psychiatric qualifications for prescribing and/or administering treatment. Interviews and conversations shall take place in such a manner as to ensure privacy and *confidentiality* of information. Every effort shall be made to obtain the *client's* views on what is happening and what he or she thinks should be done about it, including preferences regarding inpatient or outpatient treatment, if treatment is recommended.

C. *Medication Regulation*

1. Administration of medication only with a written order from a physician.
2. If responsibility for daily administration of medication is delegated to someone other than the client, complete *accuracy* in administering such medication.
3. Thorough explanation to the client of the purpose of any prescribed medication, plus description of side effects and possible long-range deleterious results.
4. Full consideration of client's opinions about and reactions to medication.

    5. Regular, periodic review of medication and adjustment whenever necessary.

    6. Accurate records noting client's medication history, including adverse reactions or any drug allergies; of special importance in case of emergency of drug overdose, up-to-date information regarding medication currently being used, with the prescribing psychiatrist's and/or physician's name(s) and telephone number(s).

    7. Cooperative effort by both psychiatrist and client to ensure that dosages prescribed are maintained at *minimum* required levels.

    8. Use of medication only as needed by the client, and not as a substitute for more active treatment methods or solely for the convenience of those who have responsibility of caring for the client.

    9. When client may be able to function optimally *without* medication, assistance to him or her in reducing dosage to zero and in learning to live medication-free.

    10. Applicable to community residential care facilities:[2] An established plan for supervision, administration, and *periodic review* of medications for all persons using psychotropic drugs. If some clients handle their own medication, the plan shall so state. In all cases, a written record for each resident shall be maintained indicating the type of medication and the name, address, and telephone number of the prescribing psychiatrist or medical doctor.

D. *Physical Health*

    1. Right to prompt and adequate treatment for any physical ailments; annual medical checkup (with particular attention directed toward nutritional needs of client); dental and other examinations and treatments as needed.

    2. Applicable to clients living in community residential care facilities:

---

[2] As defined in state or local law, with provision for frequent inspections and sufficiently severe penalties to ensure compliance by administrators of community residential care facilities. The California Community Care Facilities Act, for which regulations became effective August 31, 1975, may be a step in this direction.

a. Right to the protection of client's own health by proper attention to the health needs of others within the client's immediate environment (for example, immediate checkups for communicable disease when there is an indication that there may be a possibility of the existence of such a disease)'.

b. Encouragement and assistance in obtaining annual medical checkup and necessary medical, dental, and other professional care.

E. *Program, Treatment, and Services Evaluation by Client*
Right to offer suggestions, criticisms, and evaluations regarding any treatment programs in which the client participates. Client shall be encouraged to suggest innovative and alternative programs and services.

1. Right to express suggestions and grievances directly to providers of services.

2. Access to an independent agent or agency charged with the responsibilities of advising the client of his or her rights and how to exercise them, obtaining client input and evaluation of services, and acting as advocate for client rights and needs.

a. Protection of confidentiality of all communications of the client with this agent or agency.

b. In all facilities providing outpatient mental health services (including, especially, community residential care facilities), prominently posted notice informing client how to contact the client advocacy agent or agency (telephone number, office hours, and other pertinent information).

Two: The Right to Refuse Treatment and/or Services

Client shall have the right to give his or her express and informed consent regarding any treatment or services offered.

A. Client shall have the right to decline to participate in any treatment program, and to refuse any available services.

B. Client must be fully *informed* that he or she has the *right* to *refuse* any proposed treatment or services and to revoke consent at any time prior to treatment or between treatments.

   C. Client must be fully *informed* regarding the *nature and purpose of all treatments and services* offered. Information shall include, but not to be limited to: nature and seriousness of the illness or disability; prognosis without treatment; nature and procedures of the proposed treatment, including its intended intensity and duration; likelihood and degree of positive results expected from such treatment; nature of such results in terms of changes in the client's physical, emotional, and mental states of being, changes in overall personality and patterns of behavior, and probable duration of such changes or results; likelihood, nature, and extent and duration of possible risks or side effects, including any uncertainty or differences of professional opinion regarding such risks and any known means by which they can be alleviated or controlled; similar information concerning alternative forms of treatment and why the treatment recommended is the treatment of choice. The client, or the client's representative, shall have opportunity for consultation with independent specialists and with legal counsel. All explanations shall be given in language the client can understand. If the disability of the client is such that he or she is unable to fully *comprehend,* the necessary conditions for informed consent do not exist.
   D. If the disability of the client is such that he or she is unable to *assert* or *express* his or her right to refuse, the necessary conditions for informed consent do not exist.
   E. Decision of the client must be totally free of *coercive* elements. If the client's refusal of treatment will result in consequent reprisals or deprivations, or even inconveniences to the client, or if his or her acceptance of treatment will result in consequent rewards or special privileges, the necessary conditions for an uncoerced decision do not exist. It is recognized that the mere presence of such inconvenience or privileges will have significant bearing on the freedom with which a truly independent decision can be made.
   F. Exception to the right to give express and informed consent shall be a commitment or time-limited-evaluation situation as defined under state or local law.[3] In accordance with the

   [3] In California, under the Welfare and Institutions Code (Section

provisions of explicit, legally established criteria, the client would be taken by a duly authorized person to an appropriate psychiatric facility. As an inpatient, his or her rights then would be those applicable in that specific locality for hospitalized or otherwise institutionally confined patients.

Three: The Right to Confidentiality of Personal Records[4]

A. Strict adherance to, and vigorous enforcement of, the policy that *all information obtained in offering services to the client is confidential*—including but not limited to medical, psychiatric, and psychological care and treatment; assistance in obtaining employment, disability or insurance benefits; and residential, educational (vocational and nonvocational), placement, resocialization, counseling, and supportive services.

B. Requirement that *written express and informed consent* be obtained *before such information can be released* by any counselor, therapist, or other person offering services as an individual in private practice; outpatient clinic; community mental health center; community care facility (residential or nonresidential); placement agency; provider of aftercare services; vocational training, sheltered workshop, or educational program; or any other agency or facility engaged in providing services to the client.

C. *Exception* to the above release-signing procedure only in a *life-imperiling emergency situation* (such as drug overdose), where it is of vital importance that treatment personnel have access to all relevant information (for example, type of medication used by client).

D. *Notice* to the client of the purpose, content, and extent of the release, and of *his or her right to refuse* to give consent for

---

5150), a person can be detained for a seventy-two hour evaluation because he/she is alleged to be a danger to himself/herself or others, or is gravely disabled.

   [4] In California, this would mean explicitly extending confidentiality protections established by the Welfare and Institutions Code for *hospitalized* patients to include clients living in the *community*. These protections are generally referred to as the provisions of the Lanterman-Petris-Short Act, which is the 1968 legislation that brought them into effect.

release of information. Notice shall include the assurance that he or she will be neither rewarded in any way, direct or indirect, for signing the release nor penalized or inconvenienced in any way, direct or indirect, for not signing the release. The client's consent shall be totally free of all coercive elements.

E. Use of a *detailed and explicit release-of-information form* that shall include, but not necessarily be limited to, the following data:

1. Date release is signed and strictly defined time period to which release applies. The assumption shall be that any disclosure of information is granted on a one-time basis, unless other conditions are specifically stated in writing.

2. Name of person, agency, or facility releasing the information.

3. Name of person, agency, or facility to which the information is conveyed.

4. Type, general content, and amount of information for which release is granted.

5. Purpose for which the information is to be used and reason for transmitting the information.

6. Signature of the person responsible for the release-of-information transaction.

7. Signature of the client, who has been fully informed regarding the nature of the release and his or her rights relating thereto.

8. Statement enumerating fines and/or penalties applicable to persons who violate a client's right of confidentiality. This statement shall include but not be limited to the assertion that any divulgence of information to parties not specifically designated (for example, to employers or prospective employers when release of information to them has not been granted), or for any purposes not specifically noted, shall constitute a breach of confidentiality.

F. *Notation in the client's record* whenever information is released. Such notation shall include a copy of the signed release form.

G. *Provision for fines,* or other appropriate penalties, that may be levied against any individual who willfully and knowingly releases confidential information in violation of the client's right to privacy of personal records.

Four: The Right to Utilize Fully all Economic Rights and Benefits

A. Right to equal employment opportunities on the basis of demonstrated skills, knowledge, experience, personal adaptability, and other criteria customarily used in evaluating applicants for employment.
B. Right to receive a fair wage commensurate with the type and quality of work performed and with prevailing wage standards in the community.
C. Right to maintain his or her status as an employee entitled to just recompense whether or not the work performed is part of a work-therapy program, if the work has obvious economic value (for example, if the client's labor adds a significant contribution to the maintenance and operation of a facility, as indicated by a reduction in the facility's operating costs). "Economic reality is the test of employment. . . . So long as the institution derives any consequential benefit the economic reality test would indicate an employment relationship rather than mere therapeutic exercise" (*Souder* v. *Brennan,* U.S. District Court for the District of Columbia, Nov. 14, 1973).
   1. Participation in a work-therapy program, like participation in any other therapy, must be voluntary.
   2. Exception to the practice of paying the client for work performed shall be the programs established in social rehabilitation facilities, where the *entire structure* of the facility's program is based on the principle of voluntary cooperative enterprise and where benefits the client receives in the form of in-house programs, counseling, recreation, and the like, provide in themselves a form of recompense.
D. Right to be informed of and to receive *all* Supplemental Security Income and other benefits to which the client is entitled. Additional allowances, such as those for "unearned

income" (for example, Social Security Disability), shall be granted to all clients who are eligible to receive them.

Five: *The Right to a Humane Psychological and Physical Environment*

A. Freedom and, where necessary, *protection* from deprivation and neglect; disregard of, or disrespect for, the client's existence as a *human* being; discrimination, particularly in regard to neighborhood zoning; exploitation of either a financial or personal nature; personal harassment, humiliation, ridicule, or contempt; coercion (overt or covert); physical or mental abuse; corporal or unusual punishment (including withholding of the client's own money or the right to make telephone calls to friends or relatives as part of a "reward" program and interference in the daily functions of living such as eating and sleeping); and subjection to experimental, manipulative, or any other therapy procedures without the client's express and informed consent.

B. Opportunity to visit several residences before selecting the one that most closely meets individual needs. When the client requires it, assistance in locating and selecting the residence and help in moving (chiefly transportation). The goals shall be to give the client maximum mobility and freedom of choice in selecting his or her place of residence.

C. Explicit, written statement of residential policy regarding rate of rent and when rent is due; basic services to be provided; special charges for any optional or extra services and how and when these charges are to be paid; key, cleaning, or security deposits, if any; conditions under which refunds are made; telephone or PBX services, if applicable; time-defined prior notice of termination of occupancy by either client or landlord/administrator; time-defined prior notice of change in rent or other charges; assurance of written notice, enumerating causes, in event of eviction; provision for maid service or housekeeping responsibilities of the client; obligations of the client or special rules to be observed (for example, any special policies regarding curfew or the handling of residents' money or medications); provision of sample menus and schedules for meals, if board is provided; and other pertinent information.

D. Clean, safe, uncrowded, relatively attractive and pleasant living facilities, kept in good repair, with access to public transportation and other community resources.

E. Provision for personal privacy, in an environment that promotes dignity and self-respect.

F. A locked, safe place for personal possessions.

G. Sufficient closet and storage space to accommodate a wardrobe adequate to the needs of community living.

H. Bathing and toilet facilities that provide privacy, are clean and odor-free, are equipped with appropriate safety devices, and are *regularly* supplied with toilet tissue.

I. For those who are unable to take care of their own needs or who require assistance in dressing or grooming, attentiveness to matters of personal hygiene, including sufficient changes of bed linen.

J. Suitable facilities for doing personal laundry, ironing, and pressing.

K. Normal comforts of daily living: adequate heating, sunlight, ventilation, air conditioning where necessary, electricity, hot water, bed linen, comfortable beds and chairs, reading lamps, convenient access to telephone and television, and space for socializing with others.

L. Nutritionally balanced, fresh (not old or spoiled) food, served in an appetizing manner in pleasant surroundings. Food returned to the kitchen after a meal shall not be re-served to another client, either at the same meal or at another time. Soup left unconsumed by an individual client shall not be poured back into the pot for future use; leftover food shall not be scraped from individual plates into storage containers in order to be saved and re-served. All food shall be free of weevils, mold, and other forms of contamination.

M. Applicable to community residential care facilities: sixty days' notice regarding change in ownership, type of license, relocation, or impending revocation of license.

N. Applicable to community residential care facilities: protection against being summarily evicted.

Six: The Right to Maximum Freedom, Mobility, and Independence

A. Right to equal protection under the law; most especially, right to due process, including the services of a lawyer.

B. Right to the least restrictive setting necessary to the well-being of the client. In most cases, right to come and go at his or her own discretion. Right to be outdoors daily and, having met appropriate qualifications, to drive an automobile or other motor vehicle.

C. Right to freedom of choice in all religious matters.

D. Right to mail and receive unopened correspondence and to make and receive unmonitored telephone calls.

E. Right to control and use of his or her personal property.

F. Right to manage his or her own business and financial affairs; the right, therefore, to cash his or her Supplemental Security Income and other checks, and to manage his or her Medicaid (Medi-Cal in California) eligibility card.

G. Right to the establishment of a fair procedure for determining any limitations that may be placed upon the rights of individual clients to handle their own money (for example, cashing of checks by someone other than the client or allocation of monthly income by daily or weekly allowance instead of in a lump sum at the beginning of the month).

    1. The right to manage the client's business and financial affairs may be limited if, and only if, the client has clearly demonstrated that he or she requires assistance in dealing with financial matters.

    2. The procedure for establishing such limitations must meet minimal *due process* standards.

    3. Management of his or her money for the client must be accompanied by an independently verifiable system of record keeping.

    4. The *degree* of intervention in the client's affairs must be no

more than is actually required in accordance with his or her needs and capabilities.

H. Right to review any and all records *pertaining to the client* maintained by the landlord or residential facility administrator. Right to correct statements of personal information about the client. Right to insert in the client's records evaluatory comments regarding services and programs in which he or she is involved.

I. Right to entertain relatives and friends of the client's choice, so long as this right does not infringe upon the rights and activities of others.

J. Right to consult, on the premises of the residence, with mental health professionals, religious counselors, legal advisors, client advocates, or any other advisors whom the client deems to be of assistance.

K. Right, as a tenant who pays rent, to make reasonable suggestions and requests to the landlord or administrator (or to appropriate community care representatives) regarding the management of the residence. One widespread response to such suggestions, "If you don't like it, you can move," shall be considered unsatisfactory.

L. Applicable to community residential care facilities: right to be informed by posted notice of procedures for registering complaints, including, but not limited to, the address and telephone number of the complaint-receiving unit of the appropriate licensing office.

M. Right to the services of client advocates who will represent the client in his or her role as a consumer of mental health services, as a tenant, and as a citizen.

N. Right to organize with other clients in order to better promote and protect their consumer, tenant, and human rights.

O. Right to full participation in the life of the community, including, especially, cultural, educational, religious, community service, vocational, and recreational activities. Similarly, right to decline to participate in any or all of these activities.

P. Right to participate fully in the community political process, including not only the right to *vote* but also the right to have client and consumer needs *heard* and responded to by legislators, state and county agencies, city governing bodies, and the like. Right to have client information and suggestions given serious consideration by advisory boards, investigative committees, and other agencies specifically set up to monitor mental health services.

Q. Right to exercise the above rights without penalty or retaliation.

Seven: ***The Right to Information***

A. Right to be informed in advance of all proposed actions, decisions, or procedures that may affect the client and his or her way of life. Right to *participate* in the making of decisions vital to his or her well being—such right to include an objective hearing of the facts, assistance from counsel representing the *client's interests,* and advice from experts knowledgeable on the issues under consideration.

B. Right to be given honest, accurate information by public agencies and others who control access to data needed by the client.

C. Right to be informed concerning resources available to the client.

   1. Personal identification service such as the ID card offered by the California Department of Motor Vehicles. This card is solely for identification purposes for persons who do not drive and emphasizes the importance and convenience of proper identification in community living.

   2. Public transportation (schedules, bus lines, special all-day passes) and the telephone number to call for further information.

   3. Clinics, day care programs, resocialization centers, workshops that offer opportunities for occupational therapy and creative or artistic pursuits, vocational rehabilitation services and sheltered workshops, special educational or training programs, special recreational and sports activities.

   4. Names of psychiatrists, medical doctors, dentists, and

other professionals who accept Medicaid (Medi-Cal in California) patients. Consumers' guide to therapists.

5. Names of attorneys, sources of legal assistance, and individuals and organizations engaged in client advocacy.

6. Community organizations for people with special interests and needs, such as organizations of "former patients," local mental health advisory boards, the Mental Health Association, senior citizen groups, and local offices of the American Civil Liberties Union; self-help organizations such as Recovery, Inc., and Alcoholics Anonymous.

7. Names and addresses of publications written by and/or for "former patients." Names and addresses of alternative newspapers and publications.

8. Community events and programs, including educational opportunities, cultural activities (concerts, tours, plays, libraries, museums), and sports events.

9. Opportunities for work with volunteer, religious, and other community service organizations.

10. Sources of possible employment.

11. *General sources of information,* so that the client may become more self-sufficient in obtaining information he or she needs, including special newspaper listings, Yellow Pages, relevant agencies, the public library, and the offices of his or her legislative representatives.

D. Right to be apprised of his or her status as a consumer, tenant, and citizen who is entitled to all appropriate rights and privileges.

1. Before discharge from any inpatient psychiatric facility—state or community—the client shall be given an *oral explanation* of these rights. Most clients assimilate information more completely when it is presented verbally than if it is merely posted or handed to them in the form of a pamphlet. The client shall *also* receive a printed copy of this Bill of Rights. The Rights may be used in *predischarge discussions* as one aid in orienting the client to the community and to some of the resources that will be available. Knowing his or her rights, the client will be better able to maintain a position of dignity and independence.

2. This Bill of Rights shall be posted in a prominent place in all facilities supplying outpatient mental health services.
3. This Bill of Rights shall be posted in a prominent place in all community care facilities.
4. Upon being admitted to a community care facility, the client shall be given a copy of this Bill of Rights.

H. Richard Lamb

Epilogue

The guiding principles that underlie this book were set forth in Chapter One and then illustrated in each succeeding chapter, where we examined in detail the specifics of treatment and rehabilitation of the long-term patient. My purpose here is to enunciate these principles more formally and to look back over the book to cite examples that illustrate both the concepts and ways of putting them into practice.

Treatment should be primarily in the community and must be tailored to the needs of the discharged patient. But many critics have pointed to the woeful lack of effective treatment and the wretched conditions of many long-term patients now living "in the community." "Life was better for them in the hospitals," these critics say. "We should reopen and expand the state hospitals." We have seen that if the full range of community services described in this book are offered to long-term patients—including psychotherapy, therapeutic living situations suited to their needs, access to day treatment centers when they need it, work therapy if they want it, an opportunity to acquire social competence—then life in the community can be a vast improvement over that in any hospital. The long-term patient will then have been given an opportunity to be truly part of the community.

Research has shown that community services after hospitali-

171

zation, and not hospital treatment itself, make the difference in postdischarge community adjustment as measured by community tenure and social and vocational adjustment. Further, prolonged hospitalization of itself can cause serious problems: the fostering of dependency, regression, apathy, alienation from family and community, deterioration in work habits and skills, and loss of confidence in the ability to cope with the demands of the world.

Community mental health programs must give high priority to serving long-term patients. Providing an adequate number and range of services requires a firm belief at both administrative and staff levels that the job should be done, the resolve to do it and a willingness to give long-term patients a high priority so that sufficient funds are allocated. It has been clear as we have delineated what is involved in good community treatment and rehabilitation that these services are not cheap. Hopefully, the illusion has been shattered that closing the hospitals and moving patients into the community would save money. And, hopefully, we are seeing the end of the notion among community mental health professionals that long-term patients are somebody else's responsibility.

Long-term patients have a right to high-quality community treatment and rehabilitation. Such treatment must not be seen as something we bestow upon them to meet our own needs to feel charitable and giving. It is their right just as they must be accorded the rights and privileges of any citizen. We believe that the bill of rights as set forth by Priscilla Allen must be implemented to protect both patients' right to treatment and their civil rights. Just because one has been hospitalized, or labeled a mental patient, or sought outpatient psychiatric treatment does not mean that one has lost one's right to privacy and confidentiality, or the right to actively participate in one's own treatment, or the right to a humane psychological and physical environment, or the right not to be exploited.

Patients must receive much attention at the time of their first psychotic episode. Here, prevention of chronicity can be accomplished in many, though not all, cases. The timely use of psychotherapy, day treatment, vocational rehabilitation, and living alternatives can resolve problems and relieve pressures that would otherwise lead to ongoing stress and regression. We must recognize, however, that insofar as the person has succumbed to only the usual stresses of life (for instance the "normal" demands of adolescence, such as achieving independence from parents and preparing to become self-supporting), the chances are greater that his ego strength is low and that he will need ongoing support. On the other hand, to the extent that the person has succumbed to an unusual and overwhelming traumatic event, the chances are greater that intervention can prevent a long-term problem.

Mental health professionals and the community itself must maintain high but realistic expectations for long-term patients. Such patients' self-esteem is usually low, their fear of another failure high. Our expectations not only spur them on, but more importantly, serve as a vote of confidence that they can achieve success. We give such a vote of confidence when we tell a person he is ready to leave a day treatment center, that he can make sense out of and understand his symptoms, that he is able to handle a vocational rehabilitation program, that he is ready to move to a satellite apartment. We have seen that the expectations must be realistic; for example, a vocational program may fail if we expect too much too fast.

It is becoming clear that the whole concept of high expectations, valuable as it is, has often been misapplied. Too many long-term patients have been excluded from programs because more was expected of them than they could realistically handle. Community services must be able to assess patients' current capabilities accurately. Then they must be sufficiently flexible to tailor their programs so that expectations are set neither too high nor too low for patients at various levels of functioning. By the same token, the patient must also have realistic expectations of himself; he must learn to pace himself so that he does not try to outdistance his capabilities.

Clearly defined goals are needed in all aspects of our work with long-term patients. We have seen that in psychotherapy it is crucial to be clear whether our primary goal is to change basic character structure or to help the patient cope with the realities of his life. (Chapter Two maintains that the latter should be primary.) In the day treatment center, is the goal simple maintenance over long periods of time or is it the resolution of short-term problems? (Again, the latter should be primary.) Likewise, in the vocational workshop, we have seen that there is a direct relationship between the value of the experience and how clearly the purpose of a patient's presence there has been stated. The purpose must be clear to the workshop staff, the referring professional, and the client. Simply exposing a person to a treatment setting is an inefficient and diffuse process, as contrasted to a situation where staff and patient identify realistic goals and then set up a plan for working toward them.

No goal in working with the long-term patient is more important than giving him a sense of mastery, the feeling that he can cope with his own impulses and the demands of his environment. Not only does this goal result in a better adaptation to the world in which he has to live but also a sharp rise in his self-esteem and feelings of self-worth. This goal was the central concern of the strategy for psychotherapy set forth in Chapter Two, which concentrated on helping the patient first understand and then master his symptoms, strengthening his ego controls, and helping him deal with inappropriate guilt feelings. We have also focused on helping the long-term patient cope with work, with social situations, and with a living situation that maximizes his capability for independent living. For a person who feels helpless and overwhelmed by the demands of the world, achieving a sense of mastery is everything.

Working with the well part of the ego, another of our guiding principles, contributes vitally to the patient's ability to achieve mastery. By focusing not on pathology but rather on helping the person to develop his strengths, the well part of the personality is expanded and the ability to cope and to handle stress is enhanced.

A person's living situation should be as noninstitutional as possible, and the degree of envelopment should be the least needed. Degree of envelopment means the degree to which the facility sets limiting parameters in the number of life choices the resident is free to make for himself and the extent to which the resident is taken care of by the facility. On one hand, we have seen a growing recognition that a significant number of severely disabled persons, who present major problems in management, can survive outside of a state hospital only if there is available for them a long-term, locked, and intensively supervised community facility—namely, the therapeutic residential center. On the other hand, we have seen programs such as the Missouri Foster Community Program and satellite housing, where long-term patients are almost fully integrated into the community. We have also seen that community mental health staff can bring treatment to board and care homes and help change a repressive milieu into a therapeutic one.

Work therapy should be one of the cornerstones of community treatment of long-term patients. But, as we have seen, despite the fact that vocational rehabilitation has demonstrated its therapeutic value over and over, and even though patients place high priority on returning to work, many mental health professionals see it otherwise. Sidetracked by a preoccupation with pathology and a tendency to see work therapy as mundane and nonintellectual, many overlook the fact that work therapy has a solid theoretical base. It focuses on the well part of the ego, it emphasizes the development of mastery and a heightened feeling of self-esteem, it uses a high expectations approach, it discourages regression, it employs behavior modification techniques, it contributes to the process of delabeling in that it helps change the person's identity from patient to worker. Further, success in the area of work enhances the patient's functioning in other areas of his life and provides a pathway out of the mental health system.

Persons who have been labeled as "mental patients" need to learn and be permitted to regain the status of "normal" community residents. For instance, in the Missouri Foster Community Program, townspeople help former state hospital patients to become integrated into the community and to participate in its activities. These ex-patients are accepted by the townspeople and in time no longer feel like persons set apart. Normalization of their environment has been achieved.

Normalization of the patient's environment must always be a goal. We have seen a variety of programs designed to help patients acquire social competence, especially when patients' contact is not with mental health professionals but with regular members of the community—teachers, volunteers, and college students. Although the goal remains social rehabilitation, the interaction is not of professional to patient, but is more like what anyone in the community might experience. To the extent possible, other services should also be outside of mental health settings. Normalization of the patient's environment is a principle that should be applied by most services for long-term patients. For instance, the majority of long-term patients can benefit from a vocational setting. If their need is for a vocational workshop, then this workshop should be in an industrial neighborhood and the atmosphere as much like that of industry as possible. In the workshop, the person should be treated as a worker. He should feel like a worker, and problems not related to work should be referred to his therapist. When ready, he should be placed in skill training or a regular job. In relation to housing, satellite or scattered housing programs serve a similar purpose for those not yet capable of fully independent living. Residing in apartments or small houses scattered about the community, patients know that their living situation is to some degree supervised by a mental health agency. But at the same time, they are living, to the extent possible, like other people in the community rather than in an institutional setting. If community mental health is to fulfill its promise to long-term patients, it must do everything possible to make their life situation different from the segregated, dependency-fostering environment that was their lot in the state hospital.

Bibliography

ALLEN, P. "Care and Treatment of the Chronically Mentally Disabled in Residential Care Facilities." Article distributed at the Quarterly Meeting of the California Citizens Advisory Council. San Diego: October 1974a.

ALLEN, P. "A Consumer's View of California's Mental Health Care System." *Psychiatric Quarterly*, 1974b, *48*, 1–13.

ALLEN, P. "Clifford Beers: Toward a Realistic Sense of Hope." Address to the Annual Meeting of the California Association of Mental Health. Anaheim, Calif.: September 19, 1975.

ANTHONY, W. A. "Efficacy of Psychiatric Rehabilitation." *Psychological Bulletin*, 1972, *78*, 447–456.

APPLETON, W. S. "Mistreatment of Patients' Families by Psychiatrists." *American Journal of Psychiatry*, 1974, *131*, 655–657.

ARIETI, S. *Interpretation of Schizophrenia*. New York: Basic Books, 1974.

ARIETI, S. "Psychiatric Controversy: Man's Ethical Dimension." *American Journal of Psychiatry*, 1975, *132*, 39–42.

ARNHOFF, F. N. "Social Consequences of Policy Toward Mental Illness." *Science*, 1975, *188*, 1277–1281.

ATKINSON, R. M. "Current and Emerging Models of Residential Psychiatric Treatment, with Special Reference to the California Situation." *American Journal of Psychiatry*, 1975, *132*, 391–396.

AVIRAM, U., AND SEGAL, S. P. "Exclusion of the Mentally Ill." *Archives of General Psychiatry*, 1973, *29*, 126–131.

177

BATESON, G., JACKSON, D. D., AND HALEY, J. "Toward a Theory of Schizophrenia." *Behavioral Science,* 1956, *1,* 251–264.

BEARD, J. H., GOERTZEL, V., AND PEARCE, A. J. "The Effectiveness of Activity Group Therapy with Chronically Regressed Adult Schizophrenics." *International Journal of Group Psychotherapy,* 1958, *8,* 123–136.

BEIGEL, A., AND FEDER, S. L. "Patterns of Utilization in Partial Hospitalization." *American Journal of Psychiatry,* 1970, *126,* 1267–1274.

BELLAK, L., HURVICH, M., AND GEDIMAN, H. *Ego Functions in Schizophrenics, Neurotics and Normals.* New York: Wiley, 1973.

BROWN, G. W., BONE, M., DALISON, B., AND WING, J. K. *Schizophrenia and Social Care.* London: Oxford, 1966.

CARLSON, D. A., COLEMAN, J. V., ERRERA, P., AND HARRISON, R. W. "Problems in Treating the Lower Class Psychotic." *Archives of General Psychiatry,* 1965, *13,* 269–274.

CARMICHAEL, D. M. "Day Hospital Program with Emphasis on Translatable Skills." In R. L. Epps and L. D. Hanes (Eds.), *Day Care of Psychiatric Patients.* Springfield, Ill.: Charles C Thomas, 1964.

CROSS, K. W., HASSALL, C., AND GATH, D. "Psychiatric Day Care: The New Chronic Population?" *British Journal of Preventive and Social Medicine,* 1972, *26,* 199–204.

CUMMING, J., AND MARKSON, E. "The Impact of Mass Transfer on Patient Release." *Archives of General Psychiatry,* 1975, *32,* 804–809.

DETRE, T. P., AND JARECKI, H. G. *Modern Psychiatric Treatment.* Philadelphia: Lippincott, 1971.

EDELSON, M. *Sociotherapy and Psychotherapy.* Chicago: The University of Chicago Press, 1970.

ERICKSON, R. C., AND BACKUS, F. I. "Symptom Severity and Day Hospital Admission." *Hospital and Community Psychiatry,* 1973, *24,* 102–104.

EYSENCK, H. J. "The Effects of Psychotherapy: An Evaluation." *Journal of Consulting Psychology,* 1952, *16,* 319–324.

EYSENCK, H. J. *The Effects of Psychotherapy.* New York: Science House, 1969.

FAIRWEATHER, G. W. *Social Psychology in Treating Mental Illness.* New York: Wiley, 1964.

FAIRWEATHER, G. W., SANDERS, D. H., MAYNARD, H., AND CRESSLER, D. L.

Community Life for the Mentally Ill: An Alternative to Institutional Care. Chicago: Aldine, 1969.

FENICHEL, O. *The Psychoanalytic Theory of Neurosis.* London: Routledge, 1946.

FOWLKES, M. R. "Business as Usual—at the State Mental Hospital." *Psychiatry,* 1975, *38,* 55–64.

FOX, R. P. "Therapeutic Environments." *Archives of General Psychiatry,* 1973a, *29,* 514–517.

FOX, R. P. "Using Inpatient Staff for Aftercare of Severely Disturbed Chronic Patients." *Hospital and Community Psychiatry,* 1973b, *24,* 482–484.

GLASSCOTE, R. M., CUMMING, E., RUTMAN, I., SUSSEX, J. N., AND GLASSMAN, S. M. *Rehabilitating the Mentally Ill in the Community.* Washington, D.C.: Joint Information Service of American Psychiatric Association and National Association for Mental Health, 1971.

GOERTZEL, V. "Evaluation of Rehabilitation Programs." In H. R. Lamb, (Ed.), *Rehabilitation in Community Mental Health.* San Francisco: Jossey-Bass, 1971.

GOOTNICK, I. "The Psychiatric Day Center in the Treatment of the Chronic Schizophrenic." *American Journal of Psychiatry,* 1971, *128,* 485–488.

GOVEIA, L. H., AND TUTKO, T. A. *Psychiatric Rehabilitation in a Community Center,* Final Report of United States Public Health Service Research Grant MH 01531, National Institute of Mental Health. Santa Clara, Calif: Rehabilitation Mental Health Services, 1969.

GROUP FOR THE ADVANCEMENT OF PSYCHIATRY. *The Welfare System and Mental Health.* GAP Report No. 85, 1973, *8,* 341–377.

GUNDERSON, J. G. "Controversies About the Psychotherapy of Schizophrenia." *American Journal of Psychiatry,* 1973, *130,* 677–681.

GUNDERSON, J. G., AND MOSHER, L. R. "The Cost of Schizophrenia." *American Journal of Psychiatry,* 1975, *132,* 901–906.

HERZ, M. I., ENDICOTT, J., SPITZER, R. L., AND MESNIKOFF, A. "Day Versus Inpatient Hospitalization: A Controlled Study." *American Journal of Psychiatry,* 1971, *127,* 1371–1381.

HOGARTY, G. "The Plight of Schizophrenics in Modern Treatment Programs." *Hospital and Community Psychiatry,* 1971, *22,* 197–203.

HOGARTY, G. E., DENNIS, H., GUY, W., AND GROSS, G. M. "Who Goes

There?—A Critical Evaluation of Admissions to a Psychiatric Day Hospital." *American Journal of Psychiatry,* 1968, *124,* 934–944.

HOGARTY, G. E., AND GOLDBERG, S. C. "Drug and Sociotherapy in the Aftercare of Schizophrenic Patients." *Archives of General Psychiatry,* 1973, *28,* 54–64.

HOGARTY, G. E., GOLDBERG, S. C., SCHOOLER, N. R., AND THE COLLABORATIVE STUDY GROUP. "Drug and Sociotherapy in the Aftercare of Schizophrenic Patients III: Adjustment of Nonrelapsed Patients." *Archives of General Psychiatry,* 1974, *31,* 609–618.

HOGARTY, G. E., GOLDBERG, S. C., SCHOOLER, N. R., ULRICH, R. F., AND THE COLLABORATIVE STUDY GROUP. "Drug and Sociotherapy in the Aftercare of Schizophrenic Patients II: Two-Year Relapse Rates." *Archives of General Psychiatry,* 1974, *31,* 603–608.

KESKINER, A., AND ZALCMAN, M. "Returning to Community Life: The Foster Community Model." *Diseases of the Nervous System,* 1974, *35,* 419–426.

KESKINER, A., ZALCMAN, M. J., RUPPERT, E. H., AND ULETT, G. A. "The Foster Community: A Partnership in Psychiatric Rehabilitation." *American Journal of Psychiatry,* 1972, *129,* 283–288.

KIRK, S. A., AND THERRIEN, M. E. "Community Mental Health Myths and the Fate of Former Hospitalized Patients." *Psychiatry,* 1975, *38,* 209–217.

KNOWLES, E. S., AND BABA, R. K. *The Social Impact of Group Homes: A Study of Small Residential Service Programs in First Residential Areas.* Green Bay, Wisconsin: Green Bay Planning Commission, 1973.

LA COMMARE, P. L. "The Day Treatment Center: A Community Alternative to State Hospitalization." *Psychiatric Annals,* 1975, *5,* 178–183.

LAMB, H. R. "Aftercare for Former Day Hospital Patients." *Hospital and Community Psychiatry,* 1967a, *18,* 342–344.

LAMB, H. R. "Chronic Psychiatric Patients in the Day Hospital." *Archives of General Psychiatry,* 1967b, *17,* 615–621.

LAMB, H. R. "Coordination: The Key to Rehabilitation." *Hospital and Community Psychiatry,* 1971a, *22,* 46–47.

LAMB, H. R. (Ed.) *Rehabilitation in Community Mental Health.* San Francisco: Jossey-Bass, 1971b.

LAMB, H. R., AND EDELSON, M. B. "The Carrot and the Stick: Inducing Local Programs to Serve Long Term Patients." *Community Mental Health Journal,* 1976, *12.*

LAMB, H. R. "Treating Long-Term Schizophrenic Patients in the Community." In L. Bellak and H. H. Barten (Eds.), *Progress in Community Mental Health.* Vol. 3. New York: Brunner-Mazel, 1975.

LAMB, H. R., AND GOERTZEL, V. "The Demise of the State Hospital—A Premature Obituary?" *Archives of General Psychiatry,* 1972, *26,* 489–495.

LAMB, H. R., AND GOERTZEL, V. "Ellsworth House: A Community Alternative to Jail." *American Journal of Psychiatry,* 1974, *131,* 64–68

LAMB, H. R., AND GOERTZEL, V. "A Community Alternative to County Jail: The Hopes and the Realities." *Federal Probation,* 1975, *39,* 33–39.

LAMB, H. R., AND MACKOTA, C. "Vocational Rehabilitation Counseling: A 'Second Class' Profession?" *Journal of Rehabilitation,* 1975, *41,* 21–23.

LAMB, H. R., AND ODENHEIMER, J. "The Day Hospital." In H. R. Lamb, D. Heath, and J. J. Downing (Eds.), *Handbook of Community Mental Health Practice: The San Mateo Experience.* San Francisco: Jossey-Bass, 1969.

LANGSLEY, D. G., AND BARTER, J. T. "Treatment in the Community or State Hospital: An Evaluation." *Psychiatric Annals,* 1975, *5,* 163–170.

LIDZ, T. *The Person: His Development Throughout the Life Cycle.* New York: Basic Books, 1968.

LIDZ, T. *The Origin and Treatment of Schizophrenic Disorders.* New York: Basic Books, 1973.

LIEF, A. *The Commonsense Psychiatry of Dr. Adolph Meyer.* New York: McGraw-Hill, 1948.

LUDWIG, A. M. *Treating the Treatment Failures.* New York: Grune & Stratton, 1971.

MARMOR, J. "The Crisis of Middle Age." *Psychiatry Digest,* 1968, *29,* 17–21.

MARX, A. J., TEST, M. A., AND STEIN, L. I. "Extro-Hospital Management of Severe Mental Illness—Feasibility and Effects on Social Functioning." *Archives of General Psychiatry,* 1973, *29,* 505–511.

MAY, P. R. A. "Modifying Health-Care Services for Schizophrenic Patients." *Hospital and Community Psychiatry,* 1969, *20,* 363–368.

MENDEL, W. M. *Supportive Care.* Los Angeles: Mara Books, 1975.

Mental Health Association of Santa Clara County Newsletter, June 1975.

MESSIER, M., FINNERTY, R., BOTVIN, C. S., AND GRINSPOON, L. "A Follow-Up Study of Intensively Treated Chronic Schizophrenic Patients." *American Journal of Psychiatry,* 1969, *125,* 1123–1127.

MOLTZEN, S. "Showing the Way in San Jose." *Exchange,* 1975, *3,* 3–8.

MURPHY, H. B., ENGELSMANN, F., AND TOHENG-LAROCHE, F. "The Influence of Foster-Home Care on Psychiatric Patients." *Archives of General Psychiatry,* in press.

OGNYANOV, V., AND COWEN, L. "A Day Hospital Program for Patients in Crisis." *Hospital and Community Psychiatry,* 1974, *25,* 209–210.

OLSHANSKY, S. "Some Assumptions Challenged." *Community Mental Health Journal,* 1968, *4,* 153–156.

OLSHANSKY, S. "Eleven Myths in Vocational Rehabilitation." *Journal of Applied Rehabilitation Counseling,* 1972, *3,* 229–236.

PRIEN, R. F., COLE, J. O., BELKIN, N. F. "Relapse in Chronic Schizophrenics Following Abrupt Withdrawal of Tranquilizing Medication." *British Journal of Psychiatry,* 1968, *115,* 679–686.

RACHMAN, S. *The Effects of Psychotherapy.* Elmsford, N.Y.: Pergamon, 1972.

ROBBINS, E., AND ROBBINS, L. "Charge to the Community: Some Early Effects of a State Hospital System's Change of Policy." *American Journal of Psychiatry,* 1974, *131,* 641–645.

ROUSE, J., AND HOLMES, L. "A Model for Training Operators of Board and Care Facilities." *Exchange,* 1975, *3,* 9–15.

SAENGER, G. "Patterns of Change Among 'Treated' and 'Untreated' Patients Seen in Psychiatric Community Mental Health Clinics." *Journal of Nervous and Mental Diseases,* 1970, *150,* 37–50.

SANDALL, H., HAWLEY, T. T., AND GORDON, G. C. "The St. Louis Community Homes Program: Graduated Support for Long-Term Care." *American Journal of Psychiatry,* 1975, *132,* 617–622.

SCHROEDER, N., DAVIS, J. E., LOREI, T., AND CAFFEY, E. M. "Definition of Day Treatment Center Goals by Staff Consensus: A First Step in Treatment Evaluation." Unpublished paper, Veterans Administration, Washington, D.C., 1975.

SERBAN, G., AND GIDYNSKI, C. B. "Differentiating Criteria for Acute-Chronic Distinction in Schizophrenia." *Archives of General Psychiatry,* 1975, *32,* 705–712.

SERBAN, G., AND WOLOSHIN, G. "Relationship Between Pre- and Post-

Morbid Psychological Stress in Schizophrenics." *Psychological Reports,* 1974, *35,* 507–517.

SILBERSTEIN, S. O. "A Survey of the Mental Health Functions of the Systems of Residential Home Care for the Mentally Ill and Retarded in the Sacramento Area." Mimeographed. Sacramento, 1969.

SILVERMAN, W. H., AND VAL, E. "The Day Hospital in the Context of a Community Mental Health Program." *Community Mental Health Journal,* 1975, *11,* 82–90.

SIMON, W. B. "On Reluctance to Leave the Public Mental Hospital." *Psychiatry,* 1965, *28,* 145–156.

SMITH, W. G., KAPLAN, J., AND SIKER, D. "Community Mental Health and the Seriously Disturbed Patient." *Archives of General Psychiatry,* 1974, *30,* 693–696.

SPIEGLER, M., AND AGIGIAN, H. *Schools for Living.* New York: Brunner-Mazel, forthcoming.

STEIN, L. I., TEST, M. A., AND MARX, A. J. "Alternative to the Hospital: A Controlled Study." *American Journal of Psychiatry,* 1975, *132,* 517–522.

TEST, M. A., AND STEIN, L. I. "Training in Community Living: An In-Vivo Approach to Rehabilitation of the Markedly Impaired Patient." Paper presented at the Annual Meeting of the International Association of Psycho-Social Rehabilitation Services. Philadelphia: November 15, 1975.

URMER, A. H. "Implications of California's New Mental Health Law." *American Journal of Psychiatry,* 1975, *132,* 251–254.

WHITEHORN, J. C., AND BETZ, B. J. *Effective Psychotherapy with the Schizophrenic Patient.* New York: Jason Aronson, 1975.

WYNNE, L., AND RYCKOFF, I. "Pseudo-Mutuality in the Family Relations of Schizophrenics." *Psychiatry,* 1958, *21,* 205–220.

YALOM, I. D. "Group Therapy: A View of the Existential Position." *Frontiers of Psychiatry,* 1975, *5,* 5–11.

Index

Acquiring social competence, 12, 13, 115-129; in companion programs, 127, 128; in drop-in social centers, 125, 126; in friendship centers, 122-125; in a school setting, 115-121; using college students, 128, 129; using recreation departments and libraries, 121, 122

Advice, in individual psychotherapy, 22-25

AGIGIAN, H., 116

Aftercare planning, 48, 49, 92, 93

ALLEN, P., 1, 8, 9, 147, 148, 172

Alquist Committee, 148, 149

Alternative living arrangements, 33-55; degree of envelopment in, 11, 36, 37, 41-44, 47, 48; funding issues in regard to, 43, 44, 53; and licensing, 54; matching patients and facilities in, 47-50; and mental health ghetto, 50-53; and zoning ordinances, 51, 52; inside the mental health system, 35-55; outside the mental health system, 33-35; toward a therapeutic milieu in, 46, 47

ANTHONY, W. A., 2, 16

APPLETON, W. S., 28

ARIETI, S., 29

ARNHOFF, F. N., 3

ATKINSON, R. M., 43, 51

AVIRAM, U., 53

BABA, R. K., 52

BACKUS, F. I., 75

BARTER, J. T., 5, 52

BATESON, G., 70

BEARD, J. H., 10

BEIGEL, A., 77

BELKIN, N. F., 11

BELLAK, L., 72

BETZ, B. J., 15, 131

Bill of rights for citizens using outpatient mental health services, 3, 147-170; right to confidentiality of personal records, 161-163; right to due process, 166; right to humane psychological and physical environment, 164-166; right to information, 168-170; right to maximum freedom, mobility, and independence, 166-168; right to refuse treatment, 149, 159-161; right to utilize fully all economic rights and benefits, 163-164; statement of intent, 153

Board and care homes. *See* Residential care facilities

184

DATE DUE			
GAYLORD			PRINTED IN U.S.A.